PENGUIN

LETTERS T

DAVA SOBEL is the author of the international bestsellers *Longitude* and *Galileo's Daughter*, which won a Christopher Award and a *Los Angeles Times* Book Prize. In 2001 she received both the National Science Board's Public Service Award and the Bradford Washburn Award from the Museum of Science in Boston. She lives in East Hampton, New York.

Letters to Father

SUOR MARIA CELESTE
TO GALILEO
[1623–1633]

translated and annotated by
DAVA SOBEL

PENGUIN BOOKS

PENGUIN BOOKS
Published by the Penguin Group
Penguin Putnam Inc., 375 Hudson Street, New York, New York 10014, U.S.A.
Penguin Books Ltd, 80 Strand, London WC2R oRL, England
Penguin Books Australia Ltd, 250 Camberwell Road, Camberwell, Victoria 3124, Australia
Penguin Books Canada Ltd, 10 Alcorn Avenue, Toronto, Ontario, Canada M4V 3B2
Penguin Books India (P) Ltd, 11 Community Centre, Panchsheel Park, New Delhi - 110 017, India
Penguin Books (N.Z.) Ltd, Cnr Rosedale and Airborne Roads, Albany, Auckland, New Zealand
Penguin Books (South Africa) (Pty) Ltd, 24 Sturdee Avenue, Rosebank, Johannesburg 2196, South Africa

Penguin Books Ltd, Registered Offices:
Harmondsworth, Middlesex, England

First published in the United States of America by Walker Publishing Company, Inc. 2001
Published in Penguin Books 2003

1 3 5 7 9 10 8 6 4 2

THE LIBRARY OF CONGRESS HAS CATALOGUED THE HARDCOVER EDITION AS FOLLOWS:
Galilei, Maria Celeste, 1600–1634.
[Correspondence. English & Italian.]
Letters to father : suor Maria Celeste to Galileo, 1623–1633 / translated and annotated by Dava Sobel.
p. cm.
English and Italian.
ISBN 0-8027-1387-4 (hc.)
ISBN 0 14 24.3715 8 (pbk.)
1. Galilei, Galileo, 1564–1642—Correspondence. 2. Galilei, Maria Celeste, 1600–1634—
Correspondence. 3. Astronomer—Italy—Biography. I. Sobel, Dava. II. Title.
QB36.G2 A4 2001
520'.92—dc21
[B]   2001026572

PRINTED IN THE UNITED STATES OF AMERICA

Contents

For MOTHER MARY FRANCIS, P.C.C.,
Beloved Abbess of the Poor Clare Monastery of
Our Lady of Guadalupe in Roswell, New Mexico,
and her 18,000 sisters worldwide, who carry on
Suor Maria Celeste's tradition of cloistered prayer.

GALILEI GENEALOGY

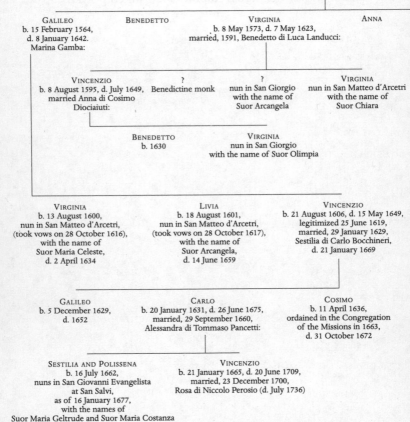

VINCENZIO
b. 1520, d. 2 July 1591,
married, 5 July 1562,
Giulia di Cosimo Ammannati
(b. 1538, d. September 1620)

GALILEO
b. 15 February 1564,
d. 8 January 1642.
Marina Gamba:

BENEDETTO

VIRGINIA
b. 8 May 1573, d. 7 May 1623,
married, 1591, Benedetto di Luca Landucci:

ANNA

VINCENZIO
b. 8 August 1595, d. July 1649,
married Anna di Cosimo
Diociaiuti:

Benedettine monk
?

nun in San Giorgio
with the name of
Suor Arcangela
?

VIRGINIA
nun in San Matteo d'Arcetri
with the name of
Suor Chiara

BENEDETTO
b. 1630

VIRGINIA
nun in San Giorgio
with the name of Suor Olimpia

VIRGINIA
b. 13 August 1600,
nun in San Matteo d'Arcetri,
(took vows on 28 October 1616),
with the name of
Suor Maria Celeste,
d. 2 April 1634

LIVIA
b. 18 August 1601,
nun in San Matteo d'Arcetri,
(took vows on 28 October 1617),
with the name of
Suor Arcangela,
d. 14 June 1659

VINCENZIO
b. 21 August 1606, d. 15 May 1649,
legitimized 25 June 1619,
married, 29 January 1629,
Sestilia di Carlo Bocchineri,
d. 21 January 1669

GALILEO
b. 5 December 1629,
d. 1652

CARLO
b. 20 January 1631, d. 26 June 1675,
married, 29 September 1660,
Alessandra di Tommaso Pancetti:

COSIMO
b. 11 April 1636,
ordained in the Congregation
of the Missions in 1663,
d. 31 October 1672

SESTILIA AND POLISSENA
b. 16 July 1662,
nuns in San Giovanni Evangelista
at San Salvi,
as of 16 January 1677,
with the names of
Suor Maria Geltrude and Suor Maria Costanza

VINCENZIO
b. 21 January 1665, d. 20 June 1709,
married, 23 December 1700,
Rosa di Niccolo Perosio (d. July 1736)

MICHELANGELO b. 18 December 1575, d. 3 January 1631, married, 1608, Anna Chiara Bandinelli (d. 1634):	LIVIA b. 7 October 1578, married, January 1601, Taddeo di Cesare Galletti	LENA (?)

	CESARE b. 15 December 1601	? b. 26 September 1603, d. 27 September 1603	GIROLAMO b. 1609	ANTONIO b. 1610

VINCENZIO b. 1608	MECHILDE d. 1634	ALBERTO CESARE b. November 1617, d. June 1692	COSIMO	MICHELANGELO d. 1634	ELISABETTA	ANNA MARIA b. 1625, d. 1634	MARIA FULVIA b. 1627, d. 1634

GALILEI FAMILY COAT OF ARMS

Introduction

The young woman who wrote these letters led a cloistered life in a gilded age. Virginia Galilei, or Suor Maria Celeste as she signs herself here, entered a convent near Florence at the age of thirteen and spent the rest of her days within its walls. Although she devoted most of her time to prayer, she served as the convent's apothecary, tended the sick nuns in the infirmary, supervised the choir, taught the novices to sing Gregorian chant, composed letters of official business for the mother abbess, wrote plays, and also performed in them. She saw as well to many personal needs of her famous father, Galileo Galilei, from mending his shirts to preparing the pastries and candies he loved to eat. When he stood trial in Rome for the crime of heresy, she managed his household affairs during the year of his absence, sending him lengthy, detailed reports at least once a week.

Had she not been Galileo's daughter, her correspondence surely would have disappeared in the lapse of centuries. But because he saved her letters, brushing them with his importance, they endure to repeat their evocative story, still speaking in the present tense, suspended in the urgency of their once current affairs.

The 124 letters span a decade, from 1623 to 1633. In that period, a pope came to power who battled the Protestant Reformation and filled Rome with artistic monuments. The Thirty Years' War embroiled all of Europe and Scandinavia. The bubonic plague erupted from Germany into Italy, where it ravaged the city of Florence until stemmed by a miracle. And a new philosophy of science threatened to overturn the order of the universe. Suor Maria Celeste's letters touch on all of these situations, but they dwell in the small details of everyday life. They tell who is sick, who has died, and who is getting well. They solicit herbs and fruits, fabric and thread. They beg for alms. They offer services, love, advice. They pray the Lord for various blessings.

Except for the time Suor Maria Celeste chides Galileo for forgetting to send the telescope he promised, she does not discuss astronomy or physics. Her letters show she follows his studies by reading his books and asking him to describe what he is working on now. More important, the letters expose a relationship that redefines Galileo's character. Through them, the legend of a brilliant innovator becomes someone's loving father; the man generally thought to have defied the Catholic Church is seen to depend on the prayers of a pious daughter.

Suor Maria Celeste probably wrote Galileo many more than just these 124 letters, as she was already twenty-two years old by the date of the first in the series. Nor is there anything in that first letter of May 10, 1623, to suggest that it initiates their epistolary relationship. Another obvious gap occurs in the year 1624, which is represented by a single letter, dated April 26, just after Galileo set off at the height of his power to visit the new pope.

"What great happiness was delivered here, Sire, along with the news of the safe progress of your journey as far as Acquasparta," this one begins, "and we hope to have even greater occasion for rejoicing when we hear tell of your arrival in Rome, where persons of grand stature most eagerly await you." Galileo stayed in Rome through early June. No doubt the long separation occasioned a stream of news to pass back and forth in writing, of which no trace remains. But it is the nature of letters to go astray. At least an appreciable sample of Suor Maria Celeste's correspondence survives. Galileo's replies, on the other hand, have disappeared.

"I set aside and save all the letters that you write me daily, Sire," Suor Maria Celeste wrote on August 13, 1623, "and whenever I find myself free, then with the greatest pleasure I reread them yet again, so that I abandon myself to thoughts of you." His half of their dialogue thus vanished through no fault of hers. Someone else must have lost or destroyed Galileo's letters.

Little is known of Suor Maria Celeste beyond what she says herself. Her birth in Padua on August 13, 1600, was recorded in a baptismal notice dated the twenty-first of that month. The announcement named her mother, "Marina of Venice," but not her father. Although Galileo and Marina Gamba never married, their twelve-year union produced a second daughter in 1601 and a son in 1606.

As a child, Virginia lived in Padua with her mother and siblings, a short walk away from the house Galileo shared with his artisans and resident students. She may have attended school, though there is no record of her having done so. Possibly she acquired her perfect grammar and literary grace from her father, who is considered a giant of Italian prose. Her mother belonged to an undistinguished family and probably never learned to read or write. But Grandmother Giulia Ammannati Galilei had gone to school as a girl in Pisa, and when Giulia took the nine-year-old Virginia home to stay with her in Florence, she may have tutored her in rhetoric.

Soon after Virginia turned ten, Galileo became philosopher and mathematician to the grand duke of Tuscany, which enabled him to move to Florence. He brought Virginia's younger sister, Livia, along with him, and father and daughters lived a while in the grandmother's lodgings. He had left the boy, Vincenzio, back in Padua, since he was only four and therefore too young to leave his mother. Galileo sent money to Marina, and kept on cordial terms with the man she ultimately married. In time he sent for Vincenzio, had him legitimized by the grand duke, and enrolled him in the University of Pisa to study law.

Galileo's decision to cloister his daughters made sense in seventeenth-century Italy. Girls from good families either got married or entered one of dozens of convents in every city. In Florence alone, fifty-three convents promised refuge and employment to girls who could not arrange a marriage, or whose families could not afford to pay dowries for every daughter. Some number of the city's four thousand nuns must have felt a true religious calling; others actively sought the cloistered life for the opportunities it offered in playwriting, poetry, and musical composition, which struck some young women as preferable to the burden of marriage and the danger of childbirth. No one knows how many girls chose the convent of their own free will, and how many pursued a "forced vocation" at their parents' insistence. Either way, a nun's work held honor and value in society. During the plague, for instance, Suor Maria Celeste's convent was enjoined by the Florentine Magistracy of Public Health to keep a forty-day prayer vigil that would help drive the pestilence out of the city.

Virginia and Livia seemed predestined for the convent life because they were both "born of fornication" (out of wedlock, though not in adultery). Galileo might have found appropriate husbands for them had he been a wealthy man, but he spread his court stipend of one thousand *scudi* per year very thin by taking care of his widowed mother, making dowry payments for his two sisters, supporting his younger brother who had a wife and too many children, and helping out needy friends and neighbors who fell on hard times.

In the autumn of 1613, Galileo took his daughters to live at the Convent of San Matteo in Arcetri, about a mile south of Florence. Determined to keep them together, he had enlisted powerful friends—cardinals—to help him defy the local law barring the admission of natural sisters into the same convent. At thirteen and twelve, Virginia and Livia were not ready to be nuns, but girls as young as nine typically boarded at convents, awaiting the day they either took the veil at the canonical age of sixteen or were taken out to be married.

Virginia adopted the name Suor Maria Celeste when she professed her nuns' vows on the feast day of Saint Francis of Assisi (October 4) in 1616. Livia became Suor Arcangela on October 28th the following year. The girls now belonged officially to the Poor Clares, the second order of Franciscans, founded by Saint Clare of Assisi in the thirteenth century.

Secluded from ordinary affairs, the Poor Clares deprived themselves of earthly comforts to pray constantly for the souls of the world. The Convent of San Matteo in Arcetri was thus destitute by design, but sometimes the virtue of poverty put the nuns' lives at risk, forcing them to appeal for outside assistance. Most of Suor Maria Celeste's letters include a request of some sort, and each such supplication is followed, a few days later, by her thanks for the items received. It appears that her father never said no to her.

At no point in these letters does Suor Maria Celeste suggest that her father's science is irreligious or that the accusations made against him are valid. Never does she hint that her position in the convent is endangered by his revolutionary ideas or his interrogation at the Holy Office of the Inquisition. On the contrary, the other nuns and their father confessor all support her and anxiously track the progress of Galileo's trial: "I greet you lovingly on behalf of all these reverend mothers, to whom every hour seems like a thousand years on account of their great desire to see you again."

She makes no mention of her real mother, who died in 1619, four years before the date of the first extant letter.

The original pages penned by Suor Maria Celeste and carried across town or between cities to Galileo are retained today among the rare manuscripts in Florence's National Central Library. They fill a hand-bound book containing letters only from women, including Galileo's mother, his younger sister, and the Tuscan ambassadress to the Vatican, though Suor Maria Celeste is by far the most frequent and the most voluble contributor. The writing paper is not only yellowed (and the ink browned), but also furrowed where the sheets were folded for mailing—pleated lengthwise into thirds or quarters, then crosswise so the edges could be sealed with red wax, and Galileo's name and address written on the outside. Although his name easily stretched out to two or more lines with honorifics—"To the Very Illustrious Lord and My Most Worthy Father, Signor Galileo Galilei"—his address was a one-word affair: "Firenze," for example, or "Roma."

Suor Maria Celeste further distinguishes herself by having folded her pages into diamond patterns, at angles to the calendered ridges of the writing paper. And although she is the only regular correspondent to endure an arduous life of obedience, chastity, silence, and poverty, her handwriting fairly erupts into frills and flourishes, far more flamboyant than the scripts of the others. It is easy to imagine her letters arriving bathed in the now lost aromas of her apothecary work—nutmeg oil for nausea, dried rhubarb and crushed roses as purgatives.

All Suor Maria Celeste's letters are first drafts, as she had neither time nor paper to waste in copying. Yet they contain only a few mistakes—a word omitted here or there, with hardly any crossing out—and the long complex sentences never lose their balance.

Her tone of voice is consistently formal, respectful, even when she treats the intimate details of medical problems or family relationships. The Italian language allows a polite form of address, and Suor Maria Celeste always employs it. She begins each letter by saluting Galileo as "Most Illustrious Lord Father" or "Most Beloved Lord Father" or "Most Illustrious and Beloved Lord Father." In the body of the letters, she calls him "V. S." for "Vostra Signoria," which can be translated as "Your Lordship" when used by one gentleman to another, or, in her case, as "Sire." Closing, she identifies herself as "Your (or Your Most Excellent Lordship's) Most Affectionate Daughter." This phraseology, which may strike the modern reader as a form of groveling, is perfectly consistent with the style of its time, when any ordinary business letter ended with the sender saying he cordially kissed the recipient's hands.

Twenty-seven of Suor Maria Celeste's letters first saw publication in Florence in 1852, in an early edition of Galileo's complete works. A free-standing collection of 121 of her letters followed in 1863, and all 124 appeared with an authoritative introduction and explanatory footnotes in 1891. Since then, Suor Maria Celeste's letters have been published more or less continually in Italy, constituting a little-known but well-loved classic of Italian literature.

Readers of English were introduced to her letters in 1870, when they served as the basis for a biography issued anonymously in London and Boston, called *A Private Life of Galileo. Compiled Principally from his Correspondence and that of his Eldest Daughter, Sister Maria Celeste, Nun in the Franciscan*

Convent of St. Matthew, in Arcetri. The author, Mary Allan-Olney, no doubt translated all the letters into English, but included only selected excerpts from them in her book.

Until now, Suor Maria Celeste's letters have never been published in their entirety in any language other than Italian.

The letters are presented here in chronological order, thanks to Suor Maria Celeste's practice of ending almost every one with a dateline, such as, "From San Matteo in Arcetri, the 8th of July 1629." Often she fixed a time by naming the corresponding Catholic holiday, writing, for example, "the feast day of San Lorenzo," because of course she knew—and Galileo knew—that day was August 10. Eight of her letters, however, bear no indication of date, and their placement here represents the best thinking of all the researchers who have been captivated by Suor Maria Celeste over the past one hundred and fifty years.

Considering how many letters of hers may have been lost or discarded, it is fortuitous and remarkable that the surviving ones chronicle the ten most tumultuous years of Galileo's life. When read alongside the testimony of his trial, or the official reports of the plague in Florence, her letters create a stirring counterpoint. Affairs of state jangle against household minutiae, and delays in the haphazard mail delivery system sometimes cause hope to rise on her end even as danger tightens around her father.

By all rights these letters should represent Suor Maria Celeste's middle years, from age twenty-two to thirty-three, but instead they mark the end of her life. The concern and responsibility she bore all through the trial of 1633 wore her down, so that the joy of Galileo's homecoming dissipated all too soon in a fatal illness, and she died during the night of April 2, 1634.

Most Illustrious Lord Father,
We are terribly saddened by the death of your cherished sister, our dear aunt [Virginia Galilei Landucci, age 50]; but our sorrow at losing her is as nothing compared to our concern for your sake, because your suffering will be all the greater, Sire, as truly you have no one else left in your world, now that she, who could not have been more precious to you, has departed, and therefore we can only imagine how you sustain the severity of such a sudden and completely unexpected blow. And while I tell you that we share deeply in your grief, you would do well to draw even greater comfort from contemplating the general state of human misery, since we are all of us here on Earth like strangers and wayfarers, who soon will be bound for our true homeland in Heaven, where there is perfect happiness, and where we must hope that your sister's blessed soul has already gone. Thus, for the love of God, we pray you, Sire, to be consoled and to put yourself in His hands, for, as you know so well, that is what He wants of you; to do otherwise would be to injure yourself and hurt us, too, because we lament grievously when we hear that you are burdened and troubled, as we have no other source of goodness in this world but you.

I will say no more, except that with all our hearts we fervently pray the Lord to comfort you and be with you always, and we greet you dearly with our ardent love.   From San Matteo, the 10th of May 1623.

Sire's Most Affectionate Daughter,
Suor M. Celeste

Most Illustrious Lord Father,
The happiness I derived from the gift of the letters you sent me,
Sire, written to you by that most distinguished Cardinal, now
elevated to the exalted position of Supreme Pontiff, was ineffable, for his letters so clearly express the affection this great man
has for you, and also show how highly he values your abilities.
[Maffeo Cardinal Barberini, long friendly to Galileo, was elected
Pope Urban VIII on August 6, 1623.] I have read and reread
them, savoring them in private, and I return them to you, as
you insist, without having shown them to anyone else except
Suor Arcangela, who has joined me in drawing the utmost joy
from seeing how much our father is favored by persons of such
caliber. May it please the Lord to grant you the robust health
you will need to fulfill your desire to visit His Holiness, so that
you can be even more greatly esteemed by him; and, seeing
how many promises he makes you in his letters, we can enter-
tain the hope that the Pope will readily grant you some sort of
assistance for our brother. In the meantime, we shall not fail to
pray the Lord, from whom all grace descends, to bless you by
letting you achieve all that you desire, so long as that be for
the best.

   I can only imagine, Sire, what a magnificent letter you must
have written to His Holiness, to congratulate him on the occasion of his reaching this exalted rank, and, because I am more
than a little bit curious, I yearn to see a copy of that letter, if it
would please you to show it, and I thank you so much for the
ones you have already sent, as well as for the melons which we
enjoyed most gratefully. I have dashed off this note in considerable haste, so I beg your pardon if I have for that reason been
sloppy or spoken amiss. I send you loving greetings along with
the others here who always ask to be remembered to you.
From San Matteo, the 10th of August.
   Sire's Most Affectionate Daughter,
   SUOR M. C.

Most Illustrious Lord Father,
It was through your most gentle and loving letter that I became fully aware of my backwardness, in assuming as I did that you, Sire, would perforce write right away to such a person, or, to put it better, to the loftiest lord in all the world. Therefore I thank you for pointing out my error, and at the same time I feel certain that you will, by the love you bear me, excuse my gross ignorance and as many other flaws as find expression in my character. I readily concede that you are the one to correct and advise me in all matters, just as I desire you to do and would so appreciate your doing, for I realize how little knowledge and ability I can justly call my own. But since, considering your continuing indisposition, we are prohibited from seeing you again for some time, we must patiently submit ourselves to the will of God, who allows everything that contributes to our well-being.

I set aside and save all the letters that you write me daily, Sire, and whenever I find myself free, then with the greatest pleasure I reread them yet again, so that I abandon myself to thoughts of you, and equally as eagerly do I anticipate reading those letters written to you by persons of distinction who feel affection for you.

Not wanting to inconvenience or bore you, I will end here, sending you warmest greetings together with Suor Arcangela and the others in our room, and Suor Diamante, too.   From San Matteo, the 13th of August 1623.

Sire's Most Affectionate Daughter,
SUOR M. CELESTE

Most Illustrious Lord Father,
This morning I learned from our steward that you find yourself ill in Florence, Sire: and because it sounds to me like something outside your normal behavior to leave home when you are troubled by your pains, I am filled with apprehension, and fear that you are in much worse condition than usual. Therefore I

beseech you to send news of yourself via this steward, so that, if you are not faring as badly as we fear, we can calm our anxious spirits. And truly I never take notice of living cloistered as a nun, except when I hear that you are sick, because then I would like to be free to come to visit and care for you with all the diligence that I could muster. But even though I cannot, I thank the Lord God for everything, knowing full well that not a leaf turns without His willing it so.

If there is anything you need, and you will only tell us what it is, we shall never fail to try to fulfill it in the very best way we know how. Meanwhile we continue, as is our custom, to pray the Lord for your coveted health, and ask that He grant you His holy grace. And I close with loving regards to you from all of us, with all our hearts.   From San Matteo, the 17th of August 1623.

 Sire's Most Affectionate Daughter,
 SUOR M. CELESTE

Most Illustrious and Beloved Lord Father,
Wishing above all else to have news of you, Sire, I dispatch our steward to you once again, and, as an excuse for the trip, I send several little fish-shaped pieces of marzipan, which, even if they do not taste quite as good as the ones you may find down along the banks of the Arno, still I think they will do you no harm, especially coming from San Matteo.

I do not, of course, mean to inconvenience or annoy you with this note, or to pressure you to write back, but only to hear a word carried from your lips about how you feel, and to learn whether there is anything we can do for you. Suor Chiara [Landucci, daughter of the recently deceased Aunt Virginia] sends her love to her father and brother as well as to you, Sire; and the two of us do the same, praying to the Lord God in our longing for your perfect health.   From San Matteo, the 21st of August 1623.

 Sire's Most Affectionate Daughter,
 SUOR M. CELESTE

We received the delicious canteloupes and watermelons, and we thank you for them.

Most Illustrious Lord Father,
We are enormously disturbed to hear that you have not improved much as yet, Sire, that on the contrary your illness has left you bedridden and stripped you of your appetite, as we learned yesterday from Master Benedetto [Landucci, her uncle]. Nonetheless we have firm hope that the Lord, through His mercy, is on the verge of restoring at least part of your health, I do not say all, as that seems almost impossible to me, considering the number of aggravations that continuously plague you, and which will undoubtedly earn you great reward and glory in the other life, since you tolerate all of this vexation with such patience.

I have searched everywhere to find you these four plums and I send them to you now, even if they are not at quite the level of perfection I would have wished; do please accept them, Sire, along with my best intentions.

Let this serve to remind you that, whenever you receive a response from those gentlemen in Rome, you did promise you would allow me to look at the letter; as for those other letters, which I know you have been meaning to let me read, I will not bother you about them now, as I imagine you do not have them with you. Not wanting to overburden you, I will say no more, except that I send you all my love together with Suor Arcangela and the others. May our Lord comfort you and be with you always.   From San Matteo, the 28th of August 1623.

Sire's Most Affectionate Daughter,
SUOR M. CELESTE

Most Illustrious and Beloved Lord Father,
I have read with tremendous pleasure the beautiful letter that
you sent to share with me. I thank you for that, and I return it
to you with the hope, however, of being able to see it again
sometime in the future, along with others and more. I enclose a
letter I have written to Vincenzio [her brother], asking you,
whenever it is convenient, to please see that it gets to him.

I give thanks to the Lord, rejoicing with you in your recovery, and I pray you to look after yourself as carefully as you
possibly can, at least until you have regained your usual level of
well-being. I thank you, too, for all the kindnesses of late, although truly, while you were ill, I almost wish you had not lav-
ished so much thoughtfulness on us. I send you every loving
greeting, together with Suor Arcangela, and I pray our Lord to
bless you with the fullness of His grace.   From San Matteo,
the last day of August 1623.

> *Sire's Most Affectionate Daughter,*
> SUOR M. CELESTE G.

Most Beloved Lord Father,
Here is the copied letter, Sire, along with the wish that it meet
with your approval, so that at other times I may again be able
to help you by my work, seeing as it gives me such great pleasure and happiness to busy myself in your service.

Madonna [the mother abbess] is not in the best position to
purchase wine just now, at least not until we have finished the
little bit we have gathered, and therefore she makes her excuses
to you accordingly, and thanks you for extending the offer even
though she is unable to accept it. The wine you sent to Suor Arcangela is perfect as far as she is concerned and she thanks you
for it: and I join her in thanking you for the thread and your
many other loving gestures.

So as not to delay the servant I will say no more, except to
send you most heartfelt greetings from all of us here and to

pray the Lord God for the fulfillment of your every desire. From San Matteo, the last day of September.

Your Most Affectionate Daughter,
SUOR M. CELESTE

Most Beloved Lord Father,
The fruits you sent were most gratefully welcomed, Sire, and as it is now a period of fasting for us Franciscans, Suor Arcangela judged them the equal of caviar; and we thank you for them.

Vincenzio stands in desperate want of more collars, even though he may not think so, as it suits him to have his used ones bleached as the need arises; but we are struggling to accommodate him in this practice, since the collars are truly old, and therefore I would like to make him four new ones with lace trim and matching cuffs; however, since I have neither the time nor the money to do this all by myself, I should like for you to make up what I lack, Sire, by sending me a *braccio* [nearly two feet] of fine cambric and at least 18 or 20 *lire* [about three *scudi*— enough money to feed a person for six weeks], to buy the lace, which my Lady Ortensia makes for me very beautifully; and because the collars worn nowadays tend to be large, they require a good deal of trimming for properly finishing them; moreover, seeing as Vincenzio has been so obedient to you, Sire, in always wearing his cuffs, I maintain, for that reason, he deserves to have handsome ones; and therefore do not be astonished that I ask for this much money. Right now I will say no more, except that I send you both my love, together with Suor Arcangela. May the Lord bless you.

Your Most Affectionate Daughter,
SUOR M. CELESTE

Most Illustrious and Beloved Lord Father,
I am returning the rest of your shirts that we have sewn, and the leather apron, too, mended as best I could. I am also sending back your letters, which are so beautifully written that they have only kindled my desire to see more examples of them. Now I am tending to the work on the linens, so that I hope you will be able to send me the trim for borders at the ends, and I remind you, Sire, that the trimming needs to be wide, because the linens themselves are rather short.

I have just placed Suor Arcangela once more into the doctor's hands, to see, with God's help, if she can be relieved of her wearisome illness, which causes me no end of worry and work.

Salvadore [Galileo's servant] tells me that you want to pay us a visit soon, Sire, which is precisely what we so desire; though I must remind you that you are obliged to keep the promise you made us, that is, to spend an entire evening here, and to be able to have dinner in the convent parlor, because we deliver the excommunication to the tablecloth and not the meals thereon [i.e. guests may bring food to share with the nuns, but cannot sit with them at table].

I enclose herewith a little composition, which, aside from expressing to you the extent of our need, will also give you the excuse to have a hearty laugh at the expense of my foolish writing; but because I have seen how good-naturedly you always encourage my meager intelligence, Sire, you have lent me the courage to attempt this essay. [The enclosure has been lost.] Indulge me then, Lord Father, and with your usual loving tenderness please help us. I thank you for the fish, and send you loving greetings along with Suor Arcangela. May our Lord grant you complete happiness.   From San Matteo, the 20th of October 1623.

Sire's Most Affectionate Daughter,
Suor M. C.

Most Illustrious and Beloved Lord Father,

If I wanted to thank you with words, Sire, for these recent presents you sent us, I could not imagine how to begin to fully express our indebtedness, and what is more, I believe that such a display of gratitude would not even please you, for, as kind and good as you are, you would prefer true thankfulness of the spirit from us over any demonstration of speeches or ceremonies. We will therefore serve you better if we apply what we do best, and by that I mean prayer, in seeking to recognize and make recompense for this and all the other innumerable, and even far greater gifts that we have received from you.

I had asked you for six yards of material, expecting to work some narrow stuff inside out and upside down, and not this expensive bolt of flannel, so large and beautiful, which will be more than enough for making the winter undergarments.

I leave you to imagine what delight I derive from reading the continuous stream of letters you send me; when I see how affectionately you share these with me, Sire, and how you enjoy making me aware of all the favors bestowed upon you by the great lords, this alone is enough to fill me to the brim with happiness. No wonder the news that you must leave so soon seems a bit harsh to me, as it means being deprived of you, and I worry that this separation will be a long one, if I am not mistaken. [Galileo plans to visit Rome for an audience with the new Pope.] And you can believe me, Sire, because I always speak the truth, that, other than you, I have no one else in this world who can console me; yet it is for this very reason that I do not grieve over your departure, any more than I would grieve over your good fortune; on the contrary, I will cheer myself, and pray and continue to pray all the while for Our Lord to grant you the soundness of body and mind to undertake this journey most prosperously, so that with the greatest contentment you can later return to us, and live happily here for many more years: may all this that I hope for you come to pass with the help of God.

I want to offer you a good word on behalf of our poor brother, although I may be speaking out of turn, yet I beseech you to forgive him his mistake this time, blaming his youth as the real cause for his committing such a blunder, which, being his first, merits pardon: I therefore entreat you once again to take him with you to Rome, and there, where you will not lack for opportunities, you can give your son the guidance that your paternal duty and all your natural goodness and loving tenderness seek to provide him.

Because I fear I may be prattling on, I will stop writing now, though I will never stop striving to remain in your good graces. And I must remind you that you still owe us the visit you have been promising for so long. Suor Arcangela and the others in the room send you a thousand regards.   From San Matteo, the 29th of October.

   Sire's Most Affectionate Daughter,
   SUOR M. CELESTE G.

Most Illustrious Lord Father,
Between the infinite love I bear you, Sire, and my fear that this sudden cold, which ordinarily troubles you so much, may aggravate your current aches and indispositions, I find it impossible to remain without news of you: therefore I beg to hear how you are, Sire, and also when you think you will be setting off on your journey. I have hastened my work on the linens, and they are almost finished; but in applying the fringe, of which I am sending you a sample, I see I will not have enough for the last two cloths, as I need almost another four *braccia* [almost three yards]. Please do everything you can to get this to me quickly, so I can send them all to you before you leave; as it is for the purpose of your upcoming trip that I have gone to such lengths to finish them.

Since I do not have a room where I can sleep through the night, Suor Diamanta, by her kindness, lets me stay in hers, depriving her own sister of that hospitality in order to take me in; but the room is terribly cold now, and with my head so infected, I cannot see how I will be able to stand it there, Sire, unless you help me by lending me one of your bed hangings, one of the white ones that you will not need to use now while you are away. I am most eager to know if you can do me this service. And another thing I ask of you, please, is to send me your book, the one that has just been published [*The Assayer*], so that I may read it, as I am longing to see what it says.

Here are some cakes I made a few days ago, hoping to give them to you when you came to bid us adieu. I see that this will not happen quite as soon as I feared, and so I want you to have them before they turn hard. Suor Arcangela continues still to purge herself, and she does not feel terribly well after having had the two cauteries on her thighs. I am still not very well either, but by now I am so accustomed to poor health that I hardly think about it, seeing how it pleases the Lord to keep testing me always with some little pain or other. I thank Him, and I pray that He grant you, Sire, the greatest possible well-being in all respects. And to close I send you loving greetings from me and from Suor Arcangela.   From San Matteo, the 21st of November 1623.

   Sire's Most Affectionate Daughter,
   S. M. CELESTE

If you have collars to be bleached, Sire, you may send them to us.

Most Illustrious and Beloved Lord Father,
I was hoping to be able to respond in person, Sire, to everything you said in your most solicitous letter of several days ago. I see, however, that time may prohibit us from meeting before you take your leave, and so I am resolved to share my thoughts with you in writing. Above all, I want you to know how happy you made me by offering so lovingly to help our convent. I conferred with Madonna and other elders here, all of whom expressed their gratitude for the nature of your offer; but because they were uncertain, not knowing how to come to a decision

among themselves, Madonna wrote to our Governor, and he answered that, since the convent is so impoverished, alms were probably needed more than anything. Meanwhile I had several discussions with one particular nun, who seems to me to surpass all the others here in wisdom and goodwill; and she, moved not by passion or self-interest but by sincere zeal, advised me, indeed beseeched me to ask you for something which would undoubtedly be of great use to us and yet very easy for you, Sire, to obtain: that is to implore His Holiness to let us have for our confessor a Regular or Brother in whom we can confide [from the Franciscan order, instead of an apprentice village priest], with the possibility that he may be replaced every three years, as is the custom at convents, by someone equally dependable; a confessor who will not interfere with the normal observances of our Order, but simply let us receive from him the Holy Sacraments: it is this that we require above all else, and so much so that I can hardly express its crucial importance, or the background circumstances that make it so, although I have tried to list several of them in the enclosed paper that I am sending along with this letter. But because I know, Sire, that you cannot, on the basis of a simple word from me, make such a demand, without hearing from others more experienced in such matters, you can look for a way, when you come here, to broach the question with Madonna, to try to get a sense of her feelings on the matter, and also to discuss it with any of the more elderly mothers, without, of course, exposing your reasons for mentioning such things. And please breathe not a word of this to Master Benedetto, since he would undoubtedly divulge it to Suor Chiara, who would then spread it among the other nuns, and thus ruin us, because it is impossible for so many brains to be of one mind; and as a consequence the actions of a single person who might be particularly displeased by this idea could thwart our efforts. Surely it would be wrong to let two or three individuals deprive everyone in the group of all the benefits, both spiritual and practical, that could accrue from the success of this plan.

Now it is up to you, Sire, with your sound judgment, to which we appeal, to determine whether you deem it appropriate to pose our entreaty, and how best to present it so as to achieve the desired end most easily; since, as far as I am concerned, our petition seems entirely legitimate, and all the more so for our being in such dire straits.

I made it a point to write to you today, Sire, as this is rather a quiet time, and I think the right time for you to come to us, before things get stirred up again, so that you can see for yourself what may need to be done in respecting the stature of the older nuns, as I have already explained.

Because I fear imposing on you too heavily, I will leave off writing here, saving all the other things to tell you later in person. Today we expect a visit from Monsignor Vicar, who is coming to attend the election of the new Abbess. May it please God to see the one who bends most to His will elected to this post, and may He grant you, Sire, an abundance of His holy grace.   From San Matteo, the 10th of December 1623.

Sire's Most Affectionate Daughter,
Suor M. Celeste G.

[The enclosed paper reads as follows:]
The first and foremost motive, which drives us to make this plea, is the clear recognition and awareness of how these priests' paltry knowledge or understanding of the orders and obligations that are part of our religious life, allow us, or, to say it better, tempt us to live ever more loosely, with scant observance of our Rule; and how can one doubt that once we begin to live without fear of God, we will be subject to continual misery with regard to the temporal matters of this world? Therefore we must address the primary cause, which is this one that I have just told you.

A second problem is that, since our convent finds itself in poverty, as you know, Sire, it cannot satisfy the confessors, who leave every three years, by giving them their salary before they go: I happen to know that three of those who were here are owed quite a large sum of money, and they use this debt as occasion to come here often to dine with us, and to fraternize with several of the nuns; and, what is worse, they then carry us in their mouths, spreading rumors and gossiping about us wherever they go, to the point where our convent is considered the concubine of the whole Casentino region, whence come these confessors of ours, more suited to hunting rabbits than guiding souls. And believe me, Sire, if I wanted to tell you all the blunders committed by the one we have with us now, I would never come to the bottom of the list, because they are as numerous as they are incredible.

The third thing will be that a Regular must never be so ignorant that he does not know much more than one of these types, or if he does not know, at least he will not flee the convent, as has been the constant practice of our priests here, on the occasion of any little happenstance, to seek advice from the bishopric or elsewhere, as though that were any way to comport oneself or counsel others; but rather he will consult some learned father of his own Order. And in this fashion our affairs will be known in only one convent, and not all over Florence, as they are now. More than this, if he has gained nothing else from his own experience, he will well understand the boundaries that a Brother must respect between himself and the nuns, in order for them to live as quietly as possible; whereas a priest who comes here without having, so to speak, knowledge of nuns, may complete the whole designated three years of his required stay without ever learning our obligations and Rule.

We are not really requesting fathers of one religious order in preference over another, trusting ourselves to the judgment of he who will obtain and grant us such a favor. It is very true that the Reformed Carmelites of Santa Maria Maggiore, who have come here many times as special confessors, have served us most satisfactorily in the offices we are prohibited from performing ourselves; and I believe that they would better conform to our need. First, being themselves very devout fathers and highly esteemed; and moreover, because they do not covet fancy gifts, nor concern themselves (being well accustomed to poverty) with a grandiose lifestyle, as members of some other Orders have sought here; certain priests sent to us as confessors spent the whole three years serving only their own interests, and the more they could wring out of us, the more skillful they considered themselves.

But, without straining to make further allegations, Sire, I

urge you to judge for yourself the conditions at other convents, such as San Jacopo and Santa Monaca, now that they have come under the influence of Brothers who took steps to set them on the proper path.

We are by no means asking to shirk the obedience of our Order, but only to be administered the Sacraments and governed by persons of experience, who appreciate the true significance of their calling.

Most Illustrious and Beloved Lord Father,
What great happiness was delivered here, Sire, along with the news (via the letter that you ordered sent to Master Benedetto) of the safe progress of your journey as far as Acquasparta, and for all of this we offer thanks to God, Master of all. We are also delighted to learn of the favors you received from Prince Cesi [Federico Cesi, Galileo's patron and publisher], and we hope to have even greater occasion for rejoicing when we hear tell of your arrival in Rome, Sire, where persons of grand stature most eagerly await you, even though I know that your joy must be tainted with considerable sorrow, on account of the sudden death of Signor Don Virginio Cesarini [Prince Cesi's young cousin, of tuberculosis], so esteemed and so loved by you. I, too, have been saddened by his passing, thinking only of the grief that you must endure, Sire, for the loss of such a dear friend, just when you stood on the verge of soon seeing him again; surely this event gives us occasion to reflect on the falsity and vanity of all hopes tied to this wretched world.

But, because I would not have you think, Sire, that I want to sermonize by letter, I will say no more, except to let you know how we fare, for I can tell you that everyone here is very well indeed, and all the nuns send you their loving regards. As for myself, I pray that our Lord grant you the fulfillment of your every just desire.   From San Matteo, the 26th of April 1624.
Sire's Most Affectionate Daughter,
SUOR M. CELESTE

Most Illustrious and Beloved Lord Father,
As for the citron, which you commanded me, Sire, to make into
candy, I have come up with only this little bit that I send you
now, because I am afraid the fruit was not fresh enough for the
confection to reach the state of perfection I would have liked,
and indeed it did not turn out very well after all. Along with
this I am sending you two baked pears for these festive days.
But to present you with an even more special gift, I enclose a
rose, which, as an extraordinary thing in this cold season, must
be warmly welcomed by you. And all the more so since, together with the rose, you will be able to accept the thorns that
represent the bitter suffering of our Lord; and also its green
leaves, symbolizing the hope that we nurture (by virtue of this
holy passion), of the reward that awaits us, after the brevity
and darkness of the winter of the present life, when at last we
will enter the clarity and happiness of the eternal spring of
Heaven, which blessed God grants us by His mercy. And ending here, I give you loving greetings, together with Suor Arcangela, and remind you, Sire, that both of us are all eagerness to
hear the current state of your health.   From San Matteo, the
19th of December 1625.
    Most Affectionate Daughter,
    SUOR M. CELESTE

I am returning the tablecloth in which you wrapped the lamb
you sent; and you, Sire, have a pillowcase of ours, which we
put over the shirts in the basket with the lid.

Most Illustrious and Beloved Lord Father,
Your having let the days go by, Sire, without coming to visit us
(this being an opportune time, as you, from what I hear, are in
command of your health, and free from demands of the Court)
would be enough to provoke some fear in me that the great
love you have always shown us may be diminishing somewhat.

Except that the expressions of your loving tenderness toward us come so frequently as to free me from this suspicion: therefore I am sooner inclined to believe that you keep putting off the visit because of the scarce satisfaction you derive from coming here, not only because the two of us, in what I suppose I would call our ineptitude, simply do not know how to show you a better time, but also because the other nuns, for other reasons, cannot keep you sufficiently amused. Given all that, I will leave off complaining, to act as though I had never entertained such thoughts; and I only pray you to bow (by allowing us to see you again) if not entirely to your own pleasure, at least partially to our wish; which would be to have you with us always, if only it were possible, in order to pay you that homage which your merits and our debt demand. Even though we are denied your presence, still we will not fail to remember our obligation to you by praising your name to the Lord so that He may grant you His grace in this life, and Paradise in the next.

I suspect that Vincenzio is complaining about us, because we lag so long in sending him the collars that he requested, insisting that he had great need of them. Please, Sire, get us a little bit of cotton batiste, so that we may sew them for him, and also give us some news of him, which we so desire. And if anything occurs to you regarding some need of yours, in which we can engage ourselves, remember that it is our greatest pleasure to serve you. And ending here, Sire, I commend myself lovingly to you, together with Suor Arcangela. From San Matteo, first day of Lent 1625. [Two months after Christmas, the year is still 1625, as the Florentine calendar begins the new year on March 25, the Feast of the Annunciation.]

Sire's Most Affectionate Daughter,
SUOR M. CELESTE

Most Illustrious and Beloved Lord Father,
Hopeful that in these most holy festivals of Christmas, and in much else besides, Sire, you will attain the summit of every

longed-for consolation, I come to you with these few lines to wish you the happiest good fortune, and I pray the Lord God, that during these blessed days your spirit enjoys quiet peace, and likewise for all the members of your household. [Galileo's sister-in-law and her children are visiting from Munich.]

I am sending a few little things for Uncle Michelangelo's children, the larger collar with the cuffs will be for Albertino, the other two for the two younger boys, and the teething bib for our baby girl, the pastry for everyone to enjoy, except the spiced cakes, as these are for you, Sire. Please also accept the good will with which I am ready to do much more.

I received the wine and also the rhubarb; I thank you; and I pray the Lord to reward you for all your loving tenderness with the fullness of His holy grace. To close I send my very loving regards to all of you.   From San Matteo, Christmas Eve 1627.
Sire's Most Affectionate Daughter,
SUOR M. CELESTE

Most Beloved Lord Father,
With the greatest happiness did I learn the other day that you fare well, Sire, although the same fortune has not followed me, as I have been confined to bed since Sunday with a fever, which (according to what the doctor says) would have been quite serious, had it not been for a sudden sweat that stopped the fever's rise and by this point has even lowered it some small amount. Now that blessed God has seen fit to keep me alive, Sire, I am availing myself of my ability, appealing to you in my neediness, confident that day after day you will minister to me with your gracious loving tenderness; and especially now that I find I must care for myself moderately well in order to overcome my extreme weakness, I would so appreciate it, Sire, if you could send me a few farthings to provide for my needs, which are so numerous that it would exhaust me just to count them, and perhaps impossible for you to assist me with them in any other fashion. I will say only that the provisions currently

given to us in the convent consist of moldy bread, ox meat, and wine that has turned sour; I enjoy your wine, of which I still have one full flask and another half, and I do not need any more just yet, because I drink so little. There is enough for me to share it with the others as is proper, and in particular with Suor Luisa, who found the last flask you sent unusually good, being so very clear, by which I mean it was of little color and great quality.

If you happen to have a hen in your poultry run that is no longer fit for laying eggs, I might make good use of her for soup, because it is helpful for me to drink weak broth. Meanwhile, not having any more to say, I send you twelve sweet pastries for you to enjoy with my love; and I send you regards together with all my companions here and the Mother Abbess, my most kind and pleasant friend. May our Lord bless you.

Your Most Affectionate Daughter,
SUOR M. CELESTE

Most Beloved Lord Father,
I truly believe that the love of a father toward his sons and daughters may be diminished somewhat, on account of the children's own bad habits or behavior; and this belief of mine grows stronger in the light of several indications you give me, Sire, for I discern a waning of the warm affection you have shown us in the past; now that you have let three months go by without coming to visit us, which feels to us like three years, and all the more worrisome, since even now that you have recovered your good health, you never write to me. I have looked within myself, to see if some error committed on my part might call down this punishment, and I do see one (albeit involuntary), which I would call a heedlessness or thoughtlessness I may give way to, when I neglect my duty to visit you and greet you more often through my letters; this particular failing of mine, accompanied as it is by my many other shortcomings, surely justifies and sustains the fear that I mentioned to you

above. Although, as I see it, my negligence should not be attributed to a weakness of my character, but rather to a lack of physical strength, precipitated by a long-standing indisposition that renders me unable to perform any of my duties; for more than a month now I have suffered headaches so severe that I could find no respite day or night. But now that my pain has abated, by the Lord's grace, I take my pen in hand to write you this long lamentation, which, in the spirit of this Carnival season, may simply be dismissed as a joke. Suffice it to say that you recall, Sire, how much we are longing to see you again, when time will allow a visit; meanwhile I send you several little treats that were given to me. They will be somewhat hard, as I have set them aside for a few days in the hope of giving them to you in person. The ring cakes are for Anna Maria and her little brothers. I enclose a letter for Vincenzio, to jog his memory that we are still alive, which he seems to have forgotten, as he never writes us a line. Lastly we send loving regards to you and our Aunt with all our hearts, and from Our Lord I pray for your true happiness.   From San Matteo, the 4th of March 1627.

 Sire's Most Affectionate Daughter,
 S. M. CELESTE

Most Beloved Lord Father,
Not knowing what in the world I might possibly send you to please you most, I thought perhaps you would like something you could present to Signora Barbera and your other caretakers, to whom I, too, confess (out of my love for you, Sire) that I am very much obliged. Therefore I send along these small pastries, for all of you to enjoy together with our love in these days of Lenten sacrifice; and if you would send us word, Sire, of whatever it is you might wish to have, you could do us no greater favor, since our hearts' desire is simply to be good to you in every way.

 Yesterday I pulled a tooth of mine that had been causing me tremendous suffering, so that now by the grace of the Lord I am free of the pain that has tormented me the last two months, although I still have the remnants of my headache. I hope, however, with the passage of time, to be relieved of this, too, if it pleases God, whom I pray to grant you, Sire, a complete recovery; and in closing I send loving regards to you, to Vincenzio, to Aunt Chiara and to everyone else at home, from Suor Arcangela and me.   From San Matteo, the 18th of March 1627.

    Sire's Most Affectionate Daughter,
    S. M. CELESTE

Most Beloved Lord Father,
Here is the cinnamon water, which I fear may not be to your liking, as it is quite freshly made. If you have no more of the distilled, you can return the carafe via our steward so that I can send you the other; and if the cooked pear pleases you, only say so, and I will secure you another; but I doubt that, considering the season, they will be very good from now on.

    Please remember me to my aunt and the whole household; I do not mention Vincenzio because I am uncertain whether he is still with you; I would very much like to hear his whereabouts and how he is faring. Be happy, Sire, in the knowledge that you will soon effect a complete cure, and be able to come and see us, fulfilling both our desire and your promise to us, and, if you think of anything you need, do tell us what it is. May Our Lord grant you His holy grace.   From San Matteo, the 22nd of March 1627.

    Sire's Most Affectionate Daughter,
    S. M. CELESTE

Most Beloved Lord Father,
Prohibited as I am from tending to you in person, despite my great desire to do so (this separation being the only difficulty I experience in cloistered life), I never fail to keep you a constant

companion in my thoughts and through my efforts to hear news of you every day; and because the steward was unable to see you the day before yesterday, I send him back today, with the excuse of delivering these two candied citron morsels. While he is there, Sire, you can let him know if you want anything from us, and whether the quince pear was at all to your liking, in which case I can furnish another. I will stop here, so as not to overburden you, though of course I never stop the flow of my loving regards, or my prayers for your perfect health, in which I am joined by Suor Arcangela and your many friends here.   The 24th of March 1627.

Your Most Affectionate Daughter,
S. M. CELESTE

Most Beloved Lord Father,
The happiness we feel at the news of your good progress in convalescence is inestimable, and with all our hearts we thank the Lord God, giver of every blessing.

So as not to transgress against your commandment, so lovingly issued, for a full account of our health, I tell you that I am following the doctor's orders by not observing Lent, and that, being already mostly toothless at my age, I will be very pleased if you can send me some fatty mutton, for surely I can manage to eat that. Suor Arcangela contents herself with picking at a few little things for her evening meal; what she would particularly appreciate is a little white wine. This much I tell you to obey you, though I for one cannot fathom how you manage, even now while you find yourself indisposed, to think so much of us and our needs; but there is nothing to be said about it except that you are our father, our most tender, loving father, upon whom, after blessed God, we rely for our every hope. May it please that same blessed Lord to keep you with us still, in the fullness of health. And closing here I send you my love.   From San Matteo, the 25th of March 1628 [first day of the new year].

Your Most Affectionate Daughter,
SUOR M. CELESTE

Most Beloved Lord Father,
The citrons that you sent me, Sire, I will transform to your taste most willingly: and in order to make them into marmalade and candies, I think I will need about two pounds of sugar, and, if you enjoy the flavor, a little bit of must [new wine]; all of this will be too expensive for me because I find myself so short of money: also if you want me to prepare you a preserve of rosemary flowers, which has been such a favorite of yours, then please send even more sugar.

We did not have the saucer you are missing; but I do believe that you have a pitcher of ours, and a little white dish.

I would rather you not preoccupy yourself so soon with concern for us; but rather attend to regaining and conserving your own health; and please, when you return home, I implore you to leave the garden to its own devices, at least until the weather improves, because I fear that this working outdoors has done you considerable harm: since I am in a hurry, I end here, and send you regards with all my heart. May the Lord grant you His blessing.

    Your Most Affectionate Daughter,
    SUOR M. CELESTE

I await the sugar as soon as possible, lest the citrons spoil, and if per chance another one should come into your hands, I would be most happy to have that, as well, to fill another need of mine, which I will tell you about in person, and I can hardly wait to do so.

Most Illustrious Lord Father,
Something in the peaceful air today gave me half a hope of seeing you again, Sire. Since you did not come, we were most pleased with the arrival of adorable little Albertino, along with our aunt, giving us news that you are well and that you will soon be here to see us; yet my delight was all but destroyed when I learned that you have already returned to your usual

labors in the garden, leaving me considerably disturbed; since the air is still quite raw, Sire, and you still weak from your recent illness, I fear this activity will do you harm. Please, Sire, do not forget so quickly the dire straits you were in, and have a little more love for yourself than for the garden; although I suppose it is not for love of the garden per se, but rather the joy you draw from it, that you put yourself at such risk. But in this season of Lent, when one is expected to make certain sacrifices, make this one, Sire: deprive yourself for a short while of the pleasure of the garden.

I wrote to you the other day to say that if by chance you had any more citrons, I would be most happy to have them and now I entreat you again, Sire, for if you could provide me with one or two, I would really be extremely pleased; if they are not your own homegrown ones, that will not matter, for what with Cavalier Marzi, who has become our Governor, due here this holy week to give us the holy water, Suor Luisa and I feel obligated to make him a gift of some of the specialties of our shop; and we were hoping to make him 4 of those delicacies he likes so much; the ones we made for you, Sire, are not yet dry, because the weather has not cooperated until today.

I send you a few preserved grapes, and 6 pine cones for the children. I thank you for the meat, and because I am feeling so well now, I expect to resume the observance of Lent next Friday, and for that reason, Sire, you must not think of sending me any more: to close I offer my loving regards to you and to my Aunt; may blessed God grant you happiness.

Your Most Affectionate Daughter,
SUOR M. CELESTE

Most Beloved Lord Father,
We thank you a thousand times (Suor Luisa and I) for the citrons that pleased us so much, partly because they came from you, and partly also because we could have had no better means of getting them.

We all enjoyed your Lenten dishes very much, and Suor Arcangela most of all. I am living in such a regimented manner, out of a desire to stay healthy, that you need not suspect any dietary infractions, Sire, and I promise I will obey your proscription against eating eggs. You can imagine how concerned I was, and how much it still means to me, that when you write back to Mechilde [Uncle Michelangelo's eldest daughter, in Munich], you thank her on our behalf and return her good wishes doubled.

I am returning the children's collars, and at the bottom of the basket there are 8 little sweetmeats, and knowing that you would want to share these with us in your loving way, we took the liberty of setting two aside for ourselves. I have also made (from the sugar you sent) a little bit each of the sour citron marmalade and the rosemary flower conserve, but they are not quite ready yet to send you.

I rejoice in the improvement of your health, and I pray our Lord to return you to a state of perfect well-being, if that be for the best. And, to end, I send you heartfelt greetings together with Suor Arcangela and Suor Luisa. (And of course we send regards to our aunt.)   The 8th of April 1628.

Your Most Affectionate Daughter,
Suor M. Celeste

Most Beloved Lord Father,
Your generosity and loving tenderness, Sire, represent the furthest possible remove from the avarice of Pappazzoni; indeed your virtue more closely recalls (if spirit could be equated with strength) that of Alexander the Great. Or better still, if it were up to me, I would compare you to the pelican, Sire, for just as he rends his heart to sustain his young, so do you, in like manner, deprive yourself of any necessity, without a thought for your own welfare, in order to cover every contingency for us, your beloved daughters. Now how could I not conclude that you are consumed by the thought of needing to send me three

or four pounds of sugar, so that I can candy the citrons you sent me? Certainly I do not fear that this preoccupation and anxiety could be strong enough to cause you any palpitation of the heart, and thus assured I have held off responding to you. Not to mention being overtaken by the doctor (just when I had set myself to writing) whom I had called because my mistress is sick again, for several days now, and it is up to me to take care of her, as well as tend the three others who are ill, with the result that I have found it impossible to discharge my regular duties, since in this instance it would have been improper to send another to take my place. Therefore excuse me, Sire, for my tardiness, and pray be good enough to fill this little flask (according to my mistress's wishes) full of your house wine: as long as it is not sour it will do, since the doctor forbids her to drink much, and ours at the convent is surely worse.

I still want to know, Sire, if you might be able to get me a few yards of that inexpensive wool cloth from Pisa, when they hold the fair there, as a favor to two poor little nuns who have asked for my help. In the event that you can do me this service, I will send you the description and eight *scudi* that they have already insisted on giving me to pay for it. Because I am very rushed I will say no more, except that I pray our Lord to grant you His holy grace, and I send my loving wishes to you, to my aunt, and to all the little rabble-rousers.   From San Matteo, the 10th of April 1628.

> *Your Most Affectionate Daughter,*
> SUOR M. CELESTE

Most Illustrious Lord Father,
The citrons you sent seem so very beautiful that I derive delight simply from beholding them, as well as from the diligence and workmanship required to prepare them properly; thus this endeavor brings me deep pleasure, and all the more so because I have occasion to employ myself in your service, Sire, which I find more agreeable than any other occupation in the world.

Here is the remaining jar of rosemary flower jam, just freshly made out of the sugar left over from the candied citrons, which I deem not quite ready yet to send to you, and the same is true for the citron marmalade, although I must say it turned out rather well.

As for the amount of sugar I need, it should fill several jars the size of this one I send you now, not less than six ounces each, although the other one I sent you held seven, and believe me I am not far wrong in my figures, even if I speak off the top of my head, as the saying goes: but surely you jest with me, Sire, for you well know I would not lie to you, especially in such a matter as this. Meanwhile, if you have emptied my three glass containers, you may return them when you send the additional flowers, so that I can refill them. And I would also like you to conduct a thorough search of your house, Sire, as it is time to make gifts of holy water, and if you were to find a few more empty bottles or vials that might do for the apothecary, I should gladly take them off your hands, for they would be most welcome here, or a few boxes: but enough, Sire, you understand me.

We made these *cantucci* [biscuits of flour, sugar, and egg whites] according to your recipe, now that Lent is over. Here, too, is some marzipan pastry for you, Sire, and four little treats for the boys. I thank you for the wine, which I shall share with *la nonna* [the mistress for whom she requested the wine] and our friends, because truly it is not my drink. I send you and Aunt all my love, and I pray the Lord to bless you.   The 19th of April.

> *Your Most Affectionate Daughter,*
> SUOR M. CELESTE

Most Beloved Lord Father,
We thank you, Sire, for your many expressions of thoughtfulness, all of which we will enjoy through your love.

The flowers that you sent, by my count, will make four jars

of jam, and, because they are very damp, we will wait for the others to arrive, since we prefer to use somewhat drier ones, and you say, Sire, that you want to send more. Right now I am about to start work on the two citrons that came from you most recently, which I believe will turn out better than the others.

I wish you great happiness for the most holy festival of Easter, this year and for many more to come, and I send you regards with all my heart together with Suor Arcangela.

Your Most Affectionate Daughter,
SUOR M. CELESTE

Most Beloved Lord Father,
Looking back over the past few days of this quiet time, and seeing that you have not yet come to us, Sire, makes me suspect that either you are not feeling very well or you have truly left for Pisa. To find out for certain, I dispatch this good woman to you, and seize the opportunity to have her carry along all the sweetmeats I have made; those five that are wrapped separately come from the two citrons you sent most recently, and I believe they will prove to be of much higher quality than the rest, since these particular citrons were the best and the freshest, and also the sugar I used was more refined, which makes the confection look whiter, and this sugar was a gift from Suor Luisa, now that I have no more of yours left. I wonder if you have forgotten, Sire, about the other flowers of rosemary, whose arrival I anticipate daily, since you said in your last letter that you would send them. I remind you now because I think they last only a short while.

And if you do go to Pisa before you come to see us, Sire, please remember the favor I asked you, regarding the fabric. I would also like for you to see if by chance you might have about your house and could send me a bit of *lucchesino* [dyed red woolen fabric] big enough to make a stomach coverlet, because now that the time has come to put away the winter blankets, I suffer greatly from having a cold and weak stomach. Since I find myself very busy I will not say more, except that I greet you with all my heart, and pray the Lord to grant you true happiness.   From San Matteo, the 28th of April 1628.

Your Most Affectionate Daughter,
SUOR M. CELESTE

Most Beloved Lord Father,
As I have not written to you in quite some time, Sire, you might easily assume I had forgotten, as in like manner I might suppose you had lost your way en route to visit us, since you have not walked that road in such a long while: but just as I know that I do not neglect writing to you for the aforesaid reason, but only on account of a constant and extreme shortage of time, of which I can never count a single hour truly mine, so in the same sense it behooves me to believe that you, not from forgetfulness, but under the pressure of other impediments leave off coming here; and this is easier to bear now that our Vincenzio visits in your stead, and we are appeased by having such a reliable source for good reports of you, all of which please me, except the part I hear about your going to the garden every morning; this news upsets me more than a little, as it seems to me that you will reap some strange and troublesome illness there, as came to pass last winter. Please renounce this recreation of yours that always repays you so ruinously; and if you will not do so out of love for yourself, then do it out of love for us, your children, who want to see you live to an advanced old age; which will not happen if you tax yourself thusly. I speak from personal experience, because every time I stay outdoors I suffer a terrible headache: think how much more harshly the air may punish you!

When Vincenzio was last here with us, Suor Chiara asked him for eight or ten Portuguese oranges; now she comes to ask them of you, Sire, if they are at all ripe, as she needs them for Monday morning.

I am returning your covered dish, with a cooked pear inside it, which I do not think will displease you, as well as this little bit of sweet almond pastry.

If you have collars to be whitened, you can send them together with that other covered basket you have of ours. I offer my loving greetings to you, Sire, and to Vincenzio, and Suor Arcangela does the same along with the others here. May the Lord grant you His holy grace.   From San Matteo, St. Martin's Day [the 11th of November] of 1628.

Sire's Most Affectionate Daughter,
Suor M. Celeste

Most Beloved Lord Father,
I should be continuously thanking blessed God, who, seeing fit to visit me with a few pains, gives me at the same time many consolations, one of which, or rather the greatest one in the world, is keeping you in my life, Sire, and keeping you, I must add, with ready willingness to help me in my every need, because truly, if I did not recognize this quality in you, I would be reluctant to annoy you so often; but to come at last to the reason why I impose upon you now, I tell you that Suor Arcangela has been sick for the past eight days, and although at the outset I made little of it, as it seemed to me just a chill, I see now that she needs to be purged; because, in addition to falling under her usual melancholy, she is also overtaken by a catarrh that affects her entire body, but especially her legs, where she has so many small red swellings that she cannot move without extreme fatigue. I know the best course for her is bleeding (now that nothing else has helped) and this is why I await the doctor this morning: but because I have no expense allowance for such a contingency, I beg you, for the love of God, to free me from my worry by sending me some money, as we are in dire need for many reasons, so numerous that I would find it too tedious to relate them all. If time allows, I would dearly welcome a visit from Vincenzio, with whom I could speak freely of my troubles, which are not trifling, coming from God.

Here is a cooked pear, from among those very beautiful ones you sent me recently. I learned this new method of cooking them that you may prefer, and I will appreciate your returning the container, as it is not mine. I close here with loving regards, and I pray the Lord to bless you.   From San Matteo, the 10th of December 1628.

Your Most Affectionate Daughter,
SUOR M. CELESTE

Most Beloved Lord Father,
I would not know how better to thank you, Sire, for so many kindnesses, if not by telling you that I pray Our Lord may reward you with the fullness of His holy grace, and make these festive days the happiest for you, not only this year but for many years to come, and finally to our Vincenzio to whom I send, for now, two collars and two pairs of new cuffs: the great want of time prohibits me from doing my very best work, and for this reason he will excuse me if the gifts are not entirely to his satisfaction: nor will I fail to make him another pair with the trim, as I promised.

Suor Arcangela is faring a bit better, even though she is confined to bed, and just now the confessor is coming to see her, so that I must not tarry a moment: please enjoy these *calicioni* [marzipan-like cake squares of sugar and almonds] this evening for a sweet treat, and here with all my heart I send my love to you both.

Your Most Affectionate Daughter,
SUOR M. CELESTE

Most Beloved Lord Father,
The unexpected news delivered here by our Vincenzio regarding the finalization of his wedding plans, and marrying into that esteemed family, has brought me such happiness that I would not know how better to express it, save to say that, as

great as is the love I bear you, Sire, equally great is the delight
I derive from your every joy, which I imagine in this instance to
be immense; and therefore I come now to rejoice with you, and
pray our Lord to protect you for a very long time, so that you
can savor those satisfactions that seem guaranteed to you by
the good qualities of your son and my brother, for whom my
affection grows stronger every day, as he appears to me to be a
calm and wise young man. [Vincenzio is betrothed to Sestilia
Bocchineri, the sixth child of a fine family from Prato with
strong connections to the Tuscan court.]

I would much rather have celebrated with you in person,
Sire, but if you would be so kind, I implore you to at least tell
me by letter how you plan to arrange your visit with Vincenzio's betrothed: meaning whether it may be well to meet in
Prato when Vincenzio goes there, or better to wait until she is
in Florence, since this is the usual formality among us sisters,
and surely, given her experience of having been in a convent,
she will know these customs. I await your resolution. And in
the meanwhile I bid you adieu from my heart.

   Your Most Affectionate Daughter,
   SUOR M. CELESTE

Most Beloved Lord Father,
It suits me to believe, Sire, that you must be extremely occupied
these days, or else you would have come to see us; wherefore,
wanting to learn more, I have resolved to write to you again,
telling you that I need not know the date of the betrothal visit
until it pleases you, Sire, being content with hearing only a few
days in advance, and also I will take advantage of your loving
offer to help me, since, with discretion, and considering my circumstances, you can easily judge that my own powers fall far
short of expressing my true feelings or giving my proper due.
Here then is a list of the more costly items that we will need for
making a platter of pastries, leaving the less expensive ingredients to me. [Her enclosed list asks for three pounds of sugar,

three also of almonds, and eight grams of fine confectioners' sugar.] After this, Sire, you will be able to see if you want me to make other dishes for you, such as savory meat pastries, and the like; because I firmly believe you would spend less this way than buying them already prepared by the grocer, and we will apply ourselves to making them with the utmost possible care.

What I want above all is for you to tell me your feelings about presenting a gift to the betrothed, because I do not want to do anything that is not to your liking, Sire. My thoughts lean toward making her a beautiful apron, so as to give her something that would be useful, and not require a great expenditure for us, since we could do all the work ourselves; not to mention that we have no idea how to make the high collars and ruffs that ladies are wearing nowadays.

I might think I had blundered, Sire, examining you on these many trifles, if I were not absolutely certain that you, in small details just as in great matters, exercise by far the soundest judgment of anyone. And therefore I leave everything to you. And to close I send you loving greetings together with Suor Arcangela and again to Vincenzio. May the Lord bless you. From San Matteo, the 4th of January 1628.

You will be able to send back with the steward the basket from the collars with the 3 covers, namely a dirty apron, a towel, and a handkerchief.

Your Most Affectionate Daughter,
SUOR M. CELESTE

Most Beloved Lord Father,
We are truly perfectly pleased with the bride, as she is cordial and gracious; but above all else what makes us most happy is the recognition of the love she bears you, Sire, because we can readily see that she will be eager to perform all those services for you that we would undertake if we were permitted to. Not that we will ever stop doing our part on your behalf, by which I mean that we will continually commend you to the Lord God,

because we are overwhelmingly committed to you, not only as daughters, but as the abandoned orphans we would be, Sire, if not for you.

Oh, if only I were capable of expressing to you my innermost thoughts! Then I could be certain that you would not doubt whether I loved you every bit as tenderly as ever a daughter loved a father: but I do not know how to convey these feelings to you in other words, if not by telling you that I love you more than myself: since, after God, the being I acknowledge most highly is you, and I perceive your good deeds toward me to be innumerable, so that I know I stand ever obliged and most willing, should the need arise, to risk my life in any sort of torment for your sake, except that which would offend His Divine Majesty.

Please, Sire, pardon me if I drive you to boredom by going on at such length, since sometimes I am transported by emotion. I did not set out to write you of these notions, but only to ask you if you could return the clock Saturday evening, as the sacristan who calls us to Matins would very much like to have it; but if you cannot, on account of the short time it has been in your hands, Sire, do not concern yourself: for it will be better to keep us waiting a little longer, if that is what you need to have it running properly again.

I would also like to know if you would be interested in making an exchange with us, namely to take back the guitar you gave us several years ago, and give us each a new breviary; as the ones we have had since the time we became nuns are all torn, these being the instruments we use every day; while the guitar is forever gathering dust and runs the risk of damage, so that I feel compelled, to avoid being rude, to send it away from here sometime soon. If you like, Sire, give me some suggestions as to what I might send you: and as for the breviaries, we do not care whether they are gilded, but just that they contain all the newly added Saints, and that they be clearly printed, because they will serve us in our old age, should we reach that point. [A nun's breviary contains prayers, psalms, hymns, feast days, and a catalog of saints.]

I had wanted to make you some rosemary flower jam, Sire,

but I am waiting for you to return one of my glass jars, because I have nothing to hold the jam; and so, if by chance you have a few empty bottles or vials lying about that are in your way, I would love to have them for the apothecary shop.

And here, to close, I send you my love together with Suor Arcangela and everyone else in the room. May Our Lord keep you in His grace.   The 22nd of March 1628.

Sire's Most Affectionate Daughter,
SUOR M. CELESTE

Most Illustrious Lord Father,
The discomfort I have endured ever since I came to live in this house, for want of a cell of my own, I know that you know, Sire, at least in part, and now I shall more clearly explain it to you, telling you that two or three years ago I was compelled by necessity to leave the one small cell we had, for which we paid our novice mistress (according to the custom we nuns observe) thirty-six *scudi,* and give it over totally to Suor Arcangela, so that (as much as possible) she could distance herself from this same mistress, who, tormented to distraction by her habitual moods, posed a threat, I feared, to Suor Arcangela, who often finds interaction with others unbearable; beyond that, Suor Arcangela's nature being very different from mine and rather eccentric, it pays for me to acquiesce to her in many things, in order to be able to live in the kind of peace and unity befitting the intense love we bear each other. As a result I spend every night in the disturbing company of the mistress (although I get through the nights easily enough with the help of the Lord, who suffers me to undergo these tribulations undoubtedly for my own good) and I pass the days practically a pilgrim, having no place whatsoever where I can retreat for one hour on my own. I do not yearn for large or very beautiful quarters, but only for a little bit of space, exactly like the tiny room that has just become available, now that a nun who desperately needs money wants to sell it; and, thanks to Suor Luisa's having spo-

ken well on my behalf, this nun prefers me over any of the others offering to buy it. But because its price is 35 *scudi*, while I have only ten, which Suor Luisa kindly gave me, plus the five I expect from my income, I cannot take possession of the room, and I rather fear I may lose it, Sire, if you do not assist me with the remaining amount, which is 20 *scudi*.

I explain this need to you, Sire, with a daughter's security and without ceremony, so as not to offend that loving tenderness I have experienced so often. I will only repeat that this is of the greatest necessity, on account of my having been reduced to the state in which I find myself, and because, loving me the way that I know you love me, and desiring my happiness, you can well imagine how this step will bring me the greatest satisfaction and pleasure, of a proper and honest sort, as all I seek is a little quiet and solitude. You might tell me, Sire, that to make up the sum I require, I could avail myself of the 30 *scudi* of yours that the convent is still holding: to which I respond (aside from the fact that I could not lay claim to that money quickly enough in this extreme case, as the nun selling the room faces dire straits) that you promised the Mother Abbess you would not ask her for those funds until such time as the convent enjoyed some relief from the constraint of constant expenditures; given all that, I do not think you will forsake me, Sire, in doing me this great charitable service, which I beg of you for the love of God, numbering myself now among the neediest paupers locked in prison, and not only needy, I say, but also ashamed, since I would not dare to speak so openly of my distress to your face: no less to Vincenzio; but only by resorting to this letter, Sire, can I appeal with every confidence, knowing that you will want and be able to help me. And here to close I send you regards with all my love, and also to Vincenzio and his bride. May the Lord bless you and keep you happy always.   From San Matteo, the 8th day of July 1629.

Sire's Most Affectionate Daughter,
Suor M. Celeste

Most Beloved Lord Father,
Now that we have back the ampule of oil with scorpions, Suor Luisa and I offer you profuse thanks. We have been wanting, for the past several days, to send you a little of our freshly made cinnamon water, which, what with the cold weather approaching, we think you must surely want to keep on hand; but we are still having trouble finding someone to deliver it to you. If you lived closer by (as I would wish) we might be spared these difficulties. But enough of that, we await the first opportunity and meanwhile we are eager to hear how La Lisabetta [a young neighbor maintained at San Matteo at Galileo's expense] is faring, and if she wants anything from us.

When you send the cloth for the collars for her and the handkerchief for our sister-in-law, Sire, do please let us see an example of one of the collars that suits her well, and likewise the Brescian cloth you promised me, out of which I will make the handkerchief: since I am extremely sleepy, I will say no more except that I am taking myself off to bed, as it is already late at night. I send you loving greetings together with Suor Luisa and Suor Arcangela, and the same to Vincenzio and his bride. May our Lord bless you.   From San Matteo, the 6th of September 1629.

   Sire's Most Affectionate Daughter,
   SUOR M. CELESTE

Most Illustrious Lord Father,
I am extremely sorry to hear of your indisposition, Sire, and all the more so because ordinarily your illnesses tend to be especially troublesome when you catch them here; and I dare to say, if I believed without a doubt that this excursion were that harmful to you, then how quickly would I consent to deprive myself of a sight so dear and desired; but in truth I put the blame on the contrary season. I beseech you to take care of yourself as well as you possibly can.

Nothing ever brought my Suor Luisa such great pleasure as seeing you take advantage (although in a small way) of our apothecary; her only fear is that the oxymel may not attain the excellence she would wish, Sire, for being of service to you. Here are V ounces of it as per your request, and if you find you need more we will be ready to provide it; and since the common practice is to mix it with syrup of citron rind, we are sending some of this, too, so you can see whether you like it: and, if anything else occurs to you, do please let us know.

Thank you for the cuttings, and should you perchance be able to spare some more, I will be most happy to have them, and still I will not neglect to send you some small loving tokens for La Porzia [Galileo's housekeeper]. I enclose a little marzipan, for you to enjoy with my love, and I give my best regards to you together with Vincenzio and my sister-in-law, and indeed I am very sad to hear that she, too, is sick in bed, and if she needs anything that I might be able to provide, I will be only too happy to do it. May Our Lord bless all of you with His holy grace.   The 10th of November 1629.

Your Most Affectionate Daughter,
S. MARIA CELESTE

Most Beloved Lord Father,
Now that the tempest of our many torments has subsided somewhat, I want to make you fully aware of the events, Sire, without leaving anything out, for in so doing I hope to ease my mind, and at the same time to be excused by you, for dashing off my last two letters so randomly, instead of writing in the proper manner. For truly I was half beside myself, shaken by the terror aroused in me and in all of us by our novice mistress, who, overpowered by those moods or frenzies of hers, tried twice in recent days to kill herself. The first time she struck her head and face against the ground with such force that she became monstrously deformed; the second time she stabbed herself thirteen times, leaving two wounds in her throat, two in

her stomach, and the others in her abdomen. I leave you to imagine, Sire, the horror that gripped us when we found her body all bloody and battered. But we were even more stupefied at how, as seriously injured as she was, she made the noise that drew us to enter her cell, asked for the confessor, and then in confession handed over to the priest the instrument she had used, so as to prevent any of us from seeing it (although, as far as we can conjecture, it was a pocket knife); thus it appears that she was crazy and cunning at the same time, and the only possible conclusion is that these are mysterious judgments of the Lord, Who still keeps her alive, when for every natural cause she should surely have died, as the wounds were all perilous ones, according to the surgeon; in the wake of these events we have guarded her continuously day and night. Now that the rest of us are recovered, by the grace of blessed God, and she is tied in her bed, albeit with the same deliriums, we continue to live in fear of some new outburst.

Beyond this travail of ours, I want to apprise you of another anxiety that has been weighing heavily on my heart. The very moment you were so kind as to send me the 20 *scudi* I had requested (I did not dare to speak freely of this in person, when you asked me recently if I had obtained the cell yet) I went with the money in my hand to find the nun who was selling it, expecting that she, being in extreme necessity, would willingly accept that money, but she simply could not resign herself to relinquishing the cell she loved so much, and since we did not reach an agreement between ourselves, nothing came of it, and I lost the chance to purchase that little room. Having assured you, Sire, that I could indeed obtain it, and then not succeeding, I became greatly troubled, not just on account of being deprived of my own space, but also because I suspected you would get upset, Sire, believing me to have said one thing and done another, though such deceit was never my intention; nor did I even want to have this money, which was causing me such grief. As it happened, the Mother Abbess was confronted at that point with certain contingencies, which I gladly helped her through, and now she, out of gratitude and kindness, has promised me the room of that nun who is sick, the one whose story I told you, Sire, whose room is large and beautiful, and while it is worth 120 *scudi* the Mother Abbess will give it to me for 80, thus doing me a particular favor, just as she has on other occasions always favored me. And because she knows full well that I cannot pay a bill of 80 *scudi,* she offers to reduce the price by the 30 *scudi* that you gave the convent some time ago, Sire, so that with your consent, which I see no reason to doubt, as this seems to me an opportunity not to be missed, I will have all that I could ever want in the way of comfort and satisfaction, which I already know to be of great importance to you. Therefore I entreat your consideration, so that I can give some response to our Mother Abbess, who will be relinquishing her office in a few days, and is currently settling her accounts.

I also want to know how you feel, Sire, now that the air is slightly more serene, and, not having anything better to send you, I offer a little poor man's candied quince, by which I mean that I prepared it with honey instead of sugar, so if it is not right for you, perhaps it will satisfy the others; I would not know what to give my sister-in-law now, in her condition. [Sestilia is pregnant and near term.] Surely if she had a taste for anything made by nuns, Sire, you would tell us, because we want so much to please her. Nor have I forgotten my obligation to La Porzia, but circumstances have prevented me from making anything as yet. Meanwhile if you have gathered the additional cuttings you promised me, Sire, I will be very happy to receive them, as I am holding off work on those I already have until the others arrive.

I must add that, as I write, the sick nun I mentioned earlier has taken such a turn that we think she is on the verge of death; in which event I will be obliged to give the remainder of the money to Madonna right away, so that she can make the necessary purchases for the funeral.

In my hands I hold the agate rosary you gave me, Sire, which is excessive and vain for me, while it seems perhaps right for my sister-in-law. Let me therefore return it to you, so you can learn if she would like to have it, and in exchange send me a few *scudi* for my present need, so that, if it please God, I believe

I really will have the full sum; and in consequence I will no longer be forced to burden you, Sire, for that is what concerns me most. But in fact I do not have, nor do I want to have, others to whom I can turn, except for you and my most faithful Suor Luisa, who wearies herself doing everything she can for me; but in the end we depend upon each other because alone we lack the strength that circumstances so often demand of us. Blessed be the Lord Who never fails to help us; by Whose love I pray you, Sire, to forgive me if I vex you too much, hoping that God Himself will reward you for all the good things you have done for us and continue to do, for which I thank you with all my heart, and I entreat you to excuse me if you find any errors here, because I do not have time to reread this long litany.   From San Matteo, the 22nd of November 1629.

Your Most Affectionate Daughter,
SUOR MARIA CELESTE

Most Beloved Lord Father,
The dread I have, Sire, that your coming here the other day has perhaps occasioned a typical recurrence of your older indisposition, urges me to send this messenger to you now, with the hope, however, that what I fear has not come to pass, but only what I wish: namely, that you feel extremely well, which unfortunately cannot be said of everyone here, since Suor Luisa's teacher, Suor Giulia, the one you saw the other day, Sire, and could not believe to be eighty years of age, on account of her strong spirit, that very evening was stricken with a sudden fever, catarrh, and pains of such gravity that the illness must surely kill her: and this has plunged Suor Luisa into extreme distress, because she has loved this teacher of hers so dearly. What's more, Suor Violante, following the doctor's recommendation, is now confined to bed with a fever; and, according to what this same doctor tells us, not much can be done or hoped for her: yesterday morning she took her medicine and we are waiting to see what happens. If you would be so kind, Sire, as

to send a flask of well-aged red wine for her, I would be most grateful, because our wine is very harsh, and I want to try, in any small way I can, to help her to the last.

I keep remembering my debt to La Porzia, and so I offer you these handkerchiefs that we have embroidered ourselves, and this braided silk belt, so that you can see if you would like to present them to her as a gift from me, or wait until you can find another length of that fine cloth; enough: you will do as you see fit in this matter, Sire. Please enjoy these fresh eggs this evening with my love, and to close I greet you with all my heart together with the others in the room. May the Lord bless you with His holy grace.   The 4th of January 1629.

Your Most Affectionate Daughter,
SUOR MARIA CELESTE

Most Beloved Lord Father,
In response to your most welcome letter, I can tell you that Suor Arcangela fares well, and I am almost better, now that your Doctor Ronconi prescribed a modicum of mild purgative, in order to try to remove an obstruction that has troubled me (aside from my usual ailments) for the past six months, and I believe that tomorrow morning I am to take an assortment of pills. I do not really suffer any particular pain; but being in this condition, something is bound to strike me. Suor Violante feels much improved, and continues purging. Suor Giulia gives us quite enough to do, as she is unable to fend for herself at all, and, every time she gets out of bed, three or four of us are required to hold her up. I cannot believe that she will survive this illness, what with the unrelenting fever and her body always emptying itself. I help her constantly, as now seems to be the time to prove my affection for Suor Luisa, by relieving her of as much of the care of Suor Giulia as I can.

Vincenzio worked on our clock for a few days, but since then it sounds worse than ever. For my part, I would judge the defect to be in the cord, which, owing to its being old, no longer glides. Still, since I am unable to fix it, I turn it over to you, so that you can diagnose its deficiency, and repair it. Perhaps the real defect was with me, in not knowing the right action to take, which is the reason I have left the counterweights attached this time, suspecting that perhaps they are not in their proper place; but I beseech you to send it back as quickly as you possibly can, because otherwise these nuns will not let me live.

Suor Brigida reminds you of the favor you promised her, namely the dowry for that poor young girl, and I would love to know if you have received from La Porzia what I asked of her. I do not mention this to press you, Sire, but only as a helpful reminder. I would also very much like to hear if the letter I wrote for Suor Maria Grazia met your expectations, Sire, because, if it were not suitable, I would attempt to correct any errors by writing another, having composed that one in a great rush, as I never find enough time even to finish my chores, and unfortunately I cannot wrench one additional hour from my sleep without seriously threatening my health.

I thank you for the use of the little mule, which I sat on this time, to save Suor Chiara the trouble of doing so, and thus show her that I want only to help her. I am returning the empty flask, as Suor Violante very much enjoyed the fine wine it contained, and she thanks you for that.

Suor Arcangela, when she saw the package of caviar that came from you the other day, felt cheated, convinced as she was that it must be the cheese from Holland you usually send at this time of year, so that, if you want her to rest easy, Sire, you will please send a little cheese before Carnival ends.

Now, seeing how I have chattered on, I would not sign off thus abruptly if I did not fear I were beginning to disturb you, or rather wear you out: therefore I close by sending all of you a thousand loving wishes, together with Suor Luisa and everyone else in the room. May the Lord bless you always.   The 21st of January 1629.

Your Most Affectionate Daughter,
SUOR MARIA CELESTE

Most Beloved Lord Father,

I know that you have heard all about my woes, Sire, from our Nora [the convent's gatekeeper]; and I was content to let her tell you, so as not to be always the bearer of bad news myself; but happily now I can say that Suor Luisa, by God's grace, is much better, and Suor Arcangela and I are extremely well: Suor Chiara reasonably so and the two old nuns their normal selves: may it please the Lord that you, too, Sire, enjoy the well-being that I desire, but dare not assume, considering the harshness of the weather: I am most eager to be assured of your good health, and meanwhile I send you these few cakes to break your fast during the long vigils of these winter nights.

Vincenzio came yesterday evening to deliver a fine pot of caviar, for which Suor Arcangela thanks you, Sire, this being her share not mine, as it does not suit me: I would much prefer to eat your soup, and a few dried figs to settle my stomach; the custom of all these years perhaps emboldens me too much; but knowing that such demands do not displease you, Sire, soothes and reassures me.

The clock that traveled back and forth between us so many times now runs beautifully, its flaw having been my fault, as I got it a little out of order; I sent it to you in a covered basket with a towel, and have not gotten either of those back; if you find them by chance about the house, Sire, please do return them. I will say no more for now, except that I send you loving regards on behalf of everyone I have mentioned here; and I pray blessed God to keep you happy always.   From San Matteo, the 19th of February 1629.

Sire's Most Affectionate Daughter,
SUOR MARIA CELESTE

Most Beloved Lord Father,

Just as I was quick to make requests of you, Sire, so in the same fashion I would surely not want to be tardy in thanking you for the loving gifts we have received, which were delivered here last Monday by my sister-in-law, namely a parcel of treats and thirteen very beautiful and delicious biscuits. We are busy enjoying them along with the awareness of your thoughtfulness and talent, Sire, for always finding the means to please us in every way. There were also some small lengths of fabric that I assume must come from La Porzia.

Because I know you like to hear that I do not sit idle, Sire, I tell you that I am kept extremely busy (aside from my usual duties) by the Mother Abbess, who, every time she needs to write to highly placed personages, such as our Governor, the Pious Workers, and people of that ilk, defers this burden to me, which is truly no trifle, considering my other responsibilities, and as a result I have no hope of obtaining the rest I need now more than ever; wherefore, to ease my labor and improve my skill, Sire, I would greatly appreciate your procuring me some books on letter writing, as you once promised, and which I know you would already have provided, if only your memory had served you.

Vincenzio came to see us yesterday morning (for perhaps the space of one hour) together with my sister-in-law and her mother, and from her we heard that you wanted to go to Rome, Sire, which put me into quite an agitated state. However, I calm myself with the thought that you would not undertake such a journey if you did not feel well enough to do so. I believe that before this comes to pass we will see each other again, and therefore I make no other comment here. Except that I send you loving regards with all my heart together with everyone in the room, and I pray the Lord to grant you His holy grace. From San Matteo, the 14th of March 1629.

Sire's Most Affectionate Daughter,
SUOR MARIA CELESTE

If you have collars to whiten you can send them to me, and please enjoy these fresh eggs with our love.

Most Beloved Lord Father,
I was hoping to convey in person, Sire, the holiday wishes I
owe you, and therefore I waited until today, the day when, seeing those hopes end vainly, I come with this letter to greet you
dearly, and to rejoice in the happy passage of the holy festival
days of Easter, as it does me good to believe that you are well
not only physically, but also spiritually, and I thank blessed
God for that. The only thing that disturbs me is the report I
hear of how assiduously you are attacking your scholarly work,
Sire, because I fear that this behavior is not without risk to
your health. And I would not want you, while seeking to im-
mortalize your fame, to cut short your life; a life held in such
reverence and treasured so preciously by us your children, and
by me in particular. Because, just as I have precedence over the
others in years, so too do I dare to claim that I precede and surpass them in my love for you, Sire. I pray you therefore not
to invite exhaustion through overexertion, so that you do no
harm to yourself and cause neither anguish nor torment to us.
I will say no more, so as not to bore you, save that I send you
the loving regards of my heart together with Suor Arcangela
and all our friends, and I pray the Lord to keep you in His
grace.   From San Matteo, the 6th of April 1630.
    Sire's Most Affectionate Daughter,
    SUOR MARIA CELESTE

Most Beloved Lord Father,
I have no doubt whatsoever of your readiness, Sire, to send me
most willingly all that I asked you for the other day; but in the
unfortunate event that your memory may have failed you, I
thought it wise to remind you of the flask of wine, the two
buttermilk cheeses, and that other item to have after the roast
meat; not lemons, or rosemary, as you said, Sire, but something
fundamental according to my tastes for tomorrow morning at
the hour when the Nuns dine. That is, we will be expecting

you, Sire, together with my sister-in-law and Vincenzio, just as you promised us. And meanwhile, praying to Our Lord for the fulfillment of your every desire, we send you loving regards. The 14th of April 1630.

Your Most Affectionate Daughter,
SUOR MARIA CELESTE

Most Beloved Lord Father,
I took the greatest delight, along with Suor Arcangela, in hearing that you are well, Sire, which matters more to me than anything else in the world. I feel reasonably, but not entirely well, since I am still taking the purgative on account of my blockage; and it is for this reason, as well as all the pressing duties to be tended to in the apothecary shop just at this juncture, that I have not written sooner to you, Sire, or to Her Ladyship the Ambassadress [Caterina Riccardi Niccolini, wife of the Tuscan ambassador to Rome]. But please pardon my negligence, and see if the enclosed letter suits the purpose; if not, I will await your correction.

Suor Arcangela and all the others fare well, except Suor Violante who struggles against her ongoing dysentery.

The Mother Abbess sends her regards to you, Sire, and reminds you of what she told you in person: that is, if chance should offer you the opportunity there in Rome to obtain some charitable help for our Monastery, to please extend yourself in this effort for the love of God and for our relief; although I must add that truly it seems an extraordinary thing to ask of people living so far away, who, when doing a good deed for someone, would prefer to favor their own neighbors and compatriots. Nonetheless I know that you know, Sire, by biding your time, how to pick the perfect moment for implementing your intentions successfully; and therefore I eagerly encourage you in this endeavor, because indeed we really are in dire need, and if it were not for the help we have received from several donations of alms, we would be at risk of starving to death; but may the Lord be ever praised, for, despite the depth of our poverty, He protects us from suffering anything other than the sorrow of the spirit, which we feel for seeing our Mother Abbess continually afflicted by our difficulties; and I for one sympathize with her a great deal, and would like to be able to help her, as I am especially fond of her. I remind you again of the relics that I requested, and so as not to tire you I will finish by sending you loving greetings, from me and from everyone here. And I pray our Lord to bless you.   From San Matteo, the 25th of May 1630.

    Sire's Most Affectionate Daughter,
    Suor Maria Celeste

Most Beloved Lord Father, [written after Galileo's return from Rome]
The very moment I was thinking of writing you a list of lamentations upon your long absence, or delay in visiting me, Sire, your loving tenderness is made manifest to me, locking my lips against complaint. I suppose I only accuse myself of being too shy and distrustful, whenever I suspect that the love you demonstrate to those in your presence, Sire, could diminish and degrade that which you bear us who are absent. I see very well that such thoughts display a vile and cowardly spirit, because with generosity I would have to persuade myself that, just as I could never cede to another in the matter of loving you, thus must you love us your daughters more than anyone else you might meet face to face; but I believe that my apprehension springs from my own lack of merit; and this explanation will have to suffice for now.

We are sorry to learn of your illness, and truly, Sire, this was the inevitable outcome of your having traveled about in the hot weather that oppresses us: I was rather astonished to hear how you were going to Florence every day. I beg you therefore to take a few days of rest, and not rush yourself here for a visit, because your health is even more dear to us than the sight of you. Meanwhile please see if by chance you have a rosary you could bring me, for I would like to send one to my Lady Ortensia, as I have not written to her in a very long time, just as I have also been remiss in not writing sooner to you, Sire, on account of still feeling oppressed by an extreme lassitude, such that drained me of the will even to move my pen, so to speak. But now that the heat has let up somewhat, I am feeling very well, by the grace of the Lord God, to whom I pray unceasingly for your health and well-being, Sire, as yours matters no less to me than my own.

We thank you for the wine and the fruits which we were even more delighted than usual to receive, and although we have been saving these few pieces of marzipan (12 in number) for when you came here, we are sending them now, so that they do not grow stale: the little cookies are for La Virginia [Galileo's grandniece, the daughter of Vincenzio Landucci]. I close by sending you loving greetings from all of us including the Mother Abbess.   From San Matteo, the 21st of July 1630.

Your Most Affectionate Daughter,
SUOR M. CELESTE

Most Beloved Lord Father,
By my good fortune it has befallen me to be able in some measure to make up for the most minor of the many mishaps you tell me have befallen you, Sire, meaning the spoiling of the two *barili* [about twenty gallons] of vinegar, in place of which I have provided these two *fiaschi* [about four quarts] which I send you now, as we had them on hand and they appear to be fine; do accept my sincere willingness, Sire, if only it were possible for me, to meet your every need.

Suor Violante, and we along with her, thank you so much for the frogs and melon, enjoying not only the gift itself, Sire, but your diligence and solicitude even more so.

Madonna yesterday morning enjoined me, Sire, saying that I must ask you whether you believe we still owe some formal thanks for the alms we received from the Grand Duke, because, as the gift was brought here to us by a workman who still remains at Barbadoro, we have not yet acknowledged its receipt; I forgot about it, and now I beseech you, Sire, to give me some guidance at your convenience, and meanwhile I hope to hear also of a good outcome to the appeal that you made yesterday morning. I send you regards from everyone, and I pray our Lord to bless you.   The 4th of September 1630.

Your Most Affectionate Daughter,
Suor M. Celeste

In the older *fiasco* of vinegar there were a few small damask roses.

Most Beloved Lord Father,
I offered no reply to your last letter, not wanting to detain your servant too long; now with more leisure, thanking you for all your loving thoughtfulness, I tell you that I took the greatest pleasure in proffering those exquisite plums to Suor Violante, seeing the happiness and gratitude that she showed me, as did Suor Luisa, too, for the two peaches you gave her, because she loves these more than all the other fruits.

I am mortified to hear that Madonna's appeal did not succeed, because I had perhaps too strong a wish that, with your assistance and favor, Sire, she would have received some good return: never mind, we shall await the outcome of that other effort in Rome.

Yesterday evening her highness the Grand Duchess sent over a beautiful doe to be presented to us, and everyone here made such merriment and so much noise when the deer was brought in, that I do not believe the hunters who caught it could have been more excited.

Now that the weather is beginning to turn cool, Suor Arcangela and I, together with our dearest friends, are planning to do our work in my cell, which is so spacious; but because the window is very high, it needs to be newly covered in a way that will admit a little more light. I would like to send it to you, Sire, meaning the windowpanes themselves, in the hope that you could help me by fitting them with waxed linen, which I believe will give us no trouble as it ages, but first I need to know if you will agree to do me this service. I do not doubt your loving attention; but because the work is rather more suited to a carpenter than a philosopher, I hesitate to ask. Therefore speak your mind freely to me on this matter, while I in the meantime send you loving greetings along with the Mother Abbess and all your friends here, and I pray blessed God to keep you in His holy grace.   From San Matteo, the 10th of September 1630.

Your Most Affectionate Daughter,
SUOR M. CELESTE

Most Beloved Lord Father,
I am heartsick and worried, Sire, imagining how disturbed you must be over the sudden death of your poor unfortunate worker. [Galileo's glassblower falls early victim to the bubonic plague epidemic that has recently invaded Florence.] I assume that you will use every possible precaution to protect yourself from the danger, and I fervently urge you to make great effort in this endeavor; I further believe that you possess remedies and preventatives proportionate to the present threat, wherefore I promise not to dwell on the subject. But still with all due respect and filial confidence I will exhort you to procure the best remedy of all, which is the grace of blessed God, by means of a thorough contrition and penitence. This, without doubt, is the most efficacious medicine, not only for the soul, but for the body as well: since, given that living happily is so crucial to the avoidance of contagious illness, what greater happiness could one secure in this life than the joy that comes of a clear and calm conscience? It is certain that when we possess this treasure we will fear neither danger nor death; and since the Lord justly chastises us with these whips, we try, with His aid, to stand ready to receive

the blow from that mighty hand, which, having magnanimously granted us the present life, retains the power to deprive
us of it at any moment and in any manner.

Please accept these few words proffered with an overflowing
heart, Sire, and also be aware of the situation in which, by the
Lord's mercy, I find myself, for I am yearning to enter the other
life, as every day I see more plainly the vanity and misery of this
one: in death I would stop offending blessed God, and I would
hope to be able to pray ever more effectively, Sire, for you. I do
not know but that this desire of mine may be too selfish. I pray
the Lord, who sees everything, to provide through His compassion what I fail to ask in my ignorance, and to grant you,
Sire, true consolation.

All of us here are in good physical health, save for Suor Violante, who is little by little wasting away: although indeed we
are burdened by penury and poverty, which take their toll on
us, still we are not made to suffer bodily harm, with the help of
the Lord.

I am eager to know if you have had any response from
Rome, regarding the alms you requested for us.

Signor Corso [Suor Giulia's brother] sent a weight of silk totaling 15 pounds, and Suor Arcangela and I have had our share
of it.

I am writing at the seventh hour [about midnight]: I shall insist that you excuse me if I make mistakes, Sire, because the day
does not contain one hour of time that is mine, since in addition to my other duties I have now been assigned to teach Gregorian chant to four young girls, and by Madonna's orders I
am responsible for the day-to-day conducting of the choir: which
last creates considerable labor for me, with my poor grasp of
the Latin language. It is certainly true that these exercises are
very much to my liking, if only I did not also have to work; yet
from all this I do derive one very good thing, which is that I
never ever sit idle for even one quarter of an hour. Except that
I require sufficient sleep to clear my head. If you would teach
me the secret you yourself employ, Sire, for getting by on so little sleep, I would be most grateful, because in the end the seven
hours that I waste sleeping seem far too many to me.

I shall say no more so as not to bore you, adding only that I give you my loving greetings together with our usual friends. From San Matteo, the 18th of October 1630.

Your Most Affectionate Daughter,
SUOR M. CELESTE

The little basket, which I sent you recently with several pastries, is not mine, and therefore I wish you to return it to me.

Most Beloved Lord Father,
I never doubted that you would find a way, Sire, to do me the favor I asked of you regarding the copy of your letter for the new Archbishop, and despite all you may say about not having turned a good deed, it will nonetheless turn out to be much better than anything I could ever have done by myself. I thank you from the bottom of my heart, and take this occasion to send you six quince pears I prepared, having heard from your own lips that they are a particular favorite of yours and yet you have not found any, for truly there is a great dearth of such fruits, as everyone knows: and on that score, if the promise made to me is honored, I believe I will be sending you another one.

I shall be most eager to learn whether Vincenzio has taken refuge in Prato: I had thought of writing him my honest opinion on this, exhorting him not to go, or at least not to leave the house unguarded; because this seems to me a truly rash act, considering all the mishaps that could occur; but, suspecting such efforts on my part to bear little fruit and cause much fuss, I let it go: and all the more do I cling to the indubitable hope that blessed God will make up through His providence what men fail to do, if not for lack of feeling, then for want of intelligence and consideration. [Vincenzio and Sestilia have fled the city to escape the plague.] I greet you with all my love together with our friends, and I accompany you always with my humble prayers.   The 28th of October 1630.

Your Most Affectionate Daughter,
SUOR M. CELESTE

Most Beloved Lord Father,
I am sure you know better than I, Sire, that tribulations are the
touchstone where we test the quality of God's love. Thus, to
whatever extent we can patiently bear the trials He doles out,
then in that same measure do we promise ourselves possession
of the treasure of His love, which comprises our every good. I
beseech you not to grasp the knife of these current troubles and
misfortunes by its sharp edge, lest you let it injure you that
way; but rather, seizing it by the blunt side, use it to excise all
the imperfections you may recognize in yourself; so that you
rise above the obstacles, and in this fashion, just as you pene-
trated the heavens with the vision of a Lyncean [a member of
the Lyncean Academy, and thus a keen observer of nature], so
will you, by piercing also through baser realms, arrive at an
awareness of the vanity and fallacy of all earthly things: seeing
and touching with your own hands the truth that neither the
love of your children, nor pleasures, honors or riches can con-
fer true contentment, being in themselves ephemeral; but that
only in blessed God, as in our final destination, can we find real
peace. Oh what joy will then be ours, when, rending this frag-
ile veil that impedes us, we revel in the glory of God face to
face! By all means let us struggle hard through these few days
of life that we have left, so as to be deserving of a blessing so
vast and everlasting. Wherefore it appears to me, my dearest
Lord Father, that you must keep to your own right path, availing yourself of opportunities as they present themselves, and
especially those that allow you to perpetuate your beneficence
toward those who repay you with ingratitude, for truly this action, being so rife with difficulty, is all the more perfect and vir-
tuous: indeed I think such behavior, far above any other virtue,
renders us in God's image, since, as we know from experience,
while we go about offending His Divine Majesty all through
the day, He responds by constantly showering us with blessings: and if He chastises us now and then, He does so for our
greater well-being, in the manner of a good father who keeps
his son in line with the whip. Something of the same seems to
be happening now in our poor city, where, spurred on as we are

by our dread of the danger hanging over us, at least we amend ourselves.

I do not know whether you have heard, Sire, of the death of Matteo Ninci, brother of our Suor Maria Teodora, who, according to what her brother Alessandro writes, had not been ill more than 3 or 4 days, and made his passage very much in God's grace, as far as could be determined. The others in the household still have their health, I believe, but they are all sorely tried by their great loss. I suspect you must feel as shocked as we do, Sire, remembering what a well-mannered youth he was, and how very lovable.

But then, not wanting to give you only the bad news, I must tell you also that the letter I wrote, on Madonna's behalf, to Monsignor Archbishop, was very well received by him, and she had a courteous reply with an offer of all his protection and aid. Similarly, two requests made last week to the Grand Duke and the Grand Duchess have both produced a good outcome, as we received from Her Highness on the morning of All Saints' Day [November 1] a donation of 300 loaves of bread, and orders that we send someone to collect a *moggio* [twenty-four bushels] of grain for us, which greatly alleviates Madonna's anxiety, for she did not have so much as a seed to sow.

Pardon me, Sire, if I annoy you excessively with my lengthy chatter, but, beyond your encouraging me through demonstrations of proof that you enjoy my letters, I consider you my *devoto* (to speak in our parlance of patron saints) in whom I confide my every thought, and share all my joys and sorrows; and, finding you always ready and willing to assist me, I ask you, not to fill all my needs, because they are too numerous, but to please see to those that are most pressing at present: for, with the chill weather coming on, I will surely grow numb with cold, unless you help by sending me a warm quilt to protect me, since the one I have now is not mine, and its owner wants to use it herself, as is only right. The one that you sent, Sire, along with the woolen blanket, I leave with Suor Arcangela, who wants to sleep alone, and I respect her wishes. But I am left with only one cotton coverlet, and if I wait until I have earned enough to buy a quilt, I will neither get one, nor survive this winter: therefore I beg this benevolence of my beloved *devoto,* who, as I know so well, will not be able to bear the thought of my suffering: and may it please the Lord (if it be for the best) to keep him with me for a long time to come, because, after he goes, I am left all alone in this world. But indeed it weighs heavily on me that I cannot offer him a proper exchange for his generous gifts! I will endeavor at least, or rather more than ever, to importune blessed God and the Most Holy Virgin that he be conducted into Paradise; and this will be the greatest reward that I can give him for all the good he has done and continues to do for me.

Here are two small jars of electuary for safeguarding against the plague. The one that has no written label is composed of dried figs, nuts, rue and salt, held together with as much honey as was needed. You may take it every morning, before eating, in a dose about the size of a walnut, followed immediately by drinking a little Greek or other good wine, and they say it provides a marvelous defense. I must admit that it has been overcooked, because we did not consider the tendency of the figs to harden. The other mixture is also to be taken by mouthful in the same manner as the first, but it has a harsher taste. If you decide to make regular use of either one, we will try to prepare them with greater skill. You say in your letter, Sire, that you mean to send me the telescope; I suppose that you have since forgotten, and therefore I remind you of it, as well as the basket in which I sent the quinces, because I am diligently working to find more of them for you. With that, to close, I send you greetings with all my heart together with our usual friends. From San Matteo, All Souls' Day [November 2] 1630.

> *Your Most Affectionate Daughter,*
> SUOR M. CELESTE

Most Beloved Lord Father,
I want to know if you are well, Sire, and so I am sending for word from you, also taking this opportunity to give you a small

quantity of the healing potion made by Abbess Orsola of Pistoia. I was able to get some as a very special favor, since, as the nuns of that convent are prohibited from giving it out, whoever obtains any clings to it like a holy relic. I implore you to take it with great faith and devotion, Sire, as the most effective preventive sent to us by Our Lord, He who works through the weakest persons in order to demonstrate all the more forcefully His majesty and power. Thus He makes Himself manifest now in this blessed nun, who started out as a poor servant girl, not even knowing how to read, yet was obliged to govern her entire monastery for many years, bringing it to the state of order it currently enjoys. I keep 4 or 5 letters from her as well as several other very inspirational writings of hers, and I have further reports about her from people deigned faithful who give clear indication of her extreme perfection and goodness. Therefore I beseech you, Sire, to put your faith in this remedy, because if you believe as strongly as you have indicated in my poor prayers, then all the more greatly can you trust in a soul so saintly, assuring yourself that by her merits you will escape every danger. With that I lovingly greet you and anxiously await receiving news of you.   The 8th of November 1630.

Your Most Affectionate Daughter,
Suor M. Celeste

Most Beloved Lord Father,
Sunday morning at the fourteenth hour [daybreak], our Suor Violante passed on to the other life; seeing how she suffered her long and debilitating illness with great patience and compliance with the will of His Divine Majesty, we can piously hope that she has gone to her salvation; and indeed for the past month she had been reduced to such a miserable state, unable even to turn over in bed by herself, and struggling so to swallow the tiniest bit of food, that death seemed almost desirable to her as the final end of all these trials; I wanted to let you know before now, Sire, but it was impossible for me to find the

time, which remains scarce even now, to write; wherefore I will say no more except that we are all well here by the mercy of God; and I want to know if the same is true of you, and of those close to you and especially of our little Galileino. [In fleeing Florence, Vincenzio and Sestilia left their infant son, nicknamed Galileino, in the care of his grandfather and a neighborhood wet nurse.]

I must also thank you for the quilt you sent me, which was really more than I deserve: I pray the Lord to reward you for all the good you have done for me and do continually, by blessing you with His holy grace in this life and granting you the glory of Paradise in the next: and here with all my heart I send you my love together with Suor Arcangela and Suor Luisa.   From San Matteo, the 26th of November 1630.

Your Most Affectionate Daughter,
SUOR M. CELESTE

Most Beloved Lord Father,
The arrival of Dame Piera [Galileo's new housekeeper] gave me indeed welcome consolation, Sire, since she assured me of your health; and in recognizing her as the prudent and considerate woman she seems to be, I feel a peace of mind that I would not otherwise find, whilst I think of you in these dangerous times, Sire, deprived of all other more beloved companionship and assistance. For all that, my thoughts stay fixed on you day and night, and many times I rue the great remove that bars me from being able to hear daily news of you, as I would so desire. Nonetheless I hope that blessed God, by His mercy, sees fit to deliver you from every grim misfortune, and so I pray Him with all my heart. And who can tell whether the presence of more plentiful society around you might not occasion greater peril? This much I know, whatever happens to us, everything proceeds from the particular providence of the Lord, and for our best: and with this thought I calm myself.

This evening we received a command from Monsignor Archbishop to set down the names of all our closest relatives, and to send them to him tomorrow, as His Most Illustrious Lordship wishes them all to take part in assisting our Convent, so that we can get through this long wintertime of want. I asked for and obtained permission from the Mother Abbess to be allowed to give you fair warning, Sire, so that you are not unduly surprised by such an act. I can say nothing else here except that I leave this affair to the Lord God, and for the rest I entrust myself to your wisdom. It would grieve me very much if you were to be overburdened by the decree; but on the other hand I know that I cannot in good conscience try to impede the succor and support of this poor, truly desolate house. The only possible rejoinder you could offer Monsignor Archbishop (on account of its being sufficiently widespread and well known) is the one I tell you here: namely that it would be a very useful and profitable matter to take out of the hands of many relatives of our nuns the two hundred *scudi* that they control of the sisters' dowries, and not only the two hundred *scudi* of capital for each one, but also the large sums of interest that have accrued to these individuals over the passing years. Among this company, as we gather, even Master Benedetto Landucci is a debtor to Suor Chiara his daughter, and I suspect that you, Sire, on account of serving as guarantor to him, no less to our Vincenzio, will be expected to pay their shares unless you are granted certain terms. By releasing the dowries, I believe that you would set about helping the Convent comfortably, and do much more than any of the relatives ever could, since so few of them are in a position to make new contributions. The intention of the Superiors is extremely good, and they help us as much as possible, but our need is too great. For my part I envy no one else in this world except the Capuchin Fathers, who live far removed from the cares and anxieties that are part and parcel of our lives as nuns, obliging us not only to pay our duty to the Convent by giving donations every year of both grain and money, but also to see to our many personal needs with earnings too meager to provide more than the barest necessities. And to tell the truth, I believe that we lose more than we gain by staying awake seven hours of the night to work, for in doing so we jeopardize our health, and waste the oil that is so expensive.

Hearing today from Dame Piera that you wanted to know if

we need anything, Sire, I lower myself to request a few *quattrini* [pence] to pay several small debts of mine that weigh on my mind. For the rest, if we have enough to sustain us, that is surely sufficient; this much the grace of God provides.

Of your coming here to see us, Sire, I hear you say nothing, and I do not importune you, because in any case it would bring us small satisfaction, not being able to speak freely for now [because of the plague precaution]. I was most eager to learn whether you liked the citron candy morsels; the ones made in the form of a quince came from a citron that I had procured with much entreaty, and at Suor Luisa's suggestion I preserved the flesh together with the rind of the same fruit, calling it total citron confection; the others I made from your citron, in the usual manner; but because I do not know which ones you may find more tasty, I shall prepare this other large citron the way I always do, unless I hear from you, wanting to spare no effort in making it exactly to your liking.

The list of items that I desire you to prepare for our apothecary, Sire, of boxes, glass vials, and such things, I explained to your servant and therefore I will not go over it again, except to add to it two white plates that you have of ours. With that I bid you goodnight, as it is now the ninth hour [roughly 2 A.M.] of the fourth night of December 1630.

Your Most Affectionate Daughter,
Suor M. Celeste

When you have been to see Monsignor Archbishop, I will be happy to hear a report.

Most Beloved Lord Father,
I see that this *tramontana* [cold north wind from the Apennines] will not allow you, Sire, to be with us as soon as you had promised me; on the contrary I doubt that you could brave it without compromising your health; however I send to see how you are, and to give you the candied citron peel, these morsels

having been made from the rind alone without the flesh of that
most beautiful citron. The other fanciful shapes are prepared
from both the flesh and the rind of the smaller fruits: but the
best of all these I believe you will find to be the big round one,
owing to the more than generous measure of sugar I heaped
into it.

I intend to make a little *ceppo* [Christmas cheer] for Virginia
and La Piera. I will be most pleased if you can send the two of
them here before the holy day, so I can give them their gifts;
and because I also want to make a little joke present for Suor
Luisa, I would love it if you could share in its preparation, Sire,
by seeing if per chance you have around your house some material that I might make into a curtain for the door of her cell;
whether it is hide or dyed cloth makes no difference to me: the
length should be three *braccia* and the width a little more than
one, to which I will add various odd trifles to make her laugh;
these would include bobbins, a string of sulphur matches for
lighting the lamps at night, wick taper, bootlaces, and other little items such as these, more than for anything else to give her,
just once, a sign of gratitude for all I feel I owe her. If you have
the things at home to do me this favor, Sire, I will be delighted,
if not, never mind trying to get them from outside, lest you risk
some peril, as I desire above all that you maintain your health,
and therefore I beg you to take care of yourself as well as you
possibly can.

I have heard nothing more yet regarding the business of
Monsignor Archbishop; please do let me know when you have
been called, Sire. With that I send you greetings from my heart
together with Suor Arcangela and our usual friends. May Our
Lord bless you.   From San Matteo, the 15th of December
1630.

Sire's Most Affectionate Daughter,
SUOR M. CELESTE

Most Beloved Lord Father,
I was hoping to see you again, Sire, before the imposition of the
quarantine; given that things have not turned out as I expected,
do please let me know how you stand with regard to your
physical health and peace of mind; as for the other necessities
of life, I feel certain that you manage comfortably on account
of having made proper provisions, or at least having the freedom of being able to break cloister to go in search of whatever
you need, as you have done in the past, which would be welcome news to me, nonetheless I do not believe that you find
much reason to stray from your beloved shelter, especially at
this season. May it please blessed God for the best of these
earnest efforts to promote the universal preservation of all, but
you above all others, Sire, as I hope will follow with divine
help: that aid never fails those who put their faith in Him; thus
it has come to pass here for us, since Our Lord has now provided a great sum of alms, namely two hundred four *scudi,* five
lire and four *crazie,* donated to us, I believe, by the Commissioners of Health following an order from their Most Serene
Highnesses, who show themselves to be extremely benevolent
toward our monastery, so much so that we will live through
this month without grieving our poor Mother Abbess, who I
believe has obtained this goodness through her constant prayers,
as well as by petitioning and pleading our cause to various
people.

From the citron that you sent me most recently, Sire, I have
made this little ring I send you now: the almond-shaped piece I
made from orange rind, for you to taste and see if you like it.
The quince pear would have been better a few days ago, but I had
no means of getting it to you. I have run out of paper, wherefore I will say no more, except that I greet you from the bottom
of my heart together with my usual companions.   The 24th
of January 1630.

    Your Most Affectionate Daughter,
    SUOR M. CELESTE

Most Illustrious and Beloved Lord Father,
The disturbance you have suffered over my indisposition shall have to be annulled, Sire, for at this moment I tell you that I feel reasonably well rid of the illness that recently came over me; as far as my long-standing blockage, however, I believe that will require an effective cure at a better time. Meanwhile I will go on taking good care of myself, as you urge me to do. In truth I would desire you to heed some of the same advice you offer me, by not immersing yourself so deeply in your studies that you jeopardize your health too markedly; for if your poor body is to serve as an instrument capable of sustaining your zest for understanding and investigating novelties, it is well that you grant it some needed rest, lest it become so depleted as to render even your powerful intellect unable to savor that nourishment it devours with such relish.

I will thank you not only for the two *scudi* and other loving tokens you sent me, Sire, but also for the readiness and generosity by which you show yourself ever more willing to help me, as needy as I am of being helped.

I am delighted to hear of the good health of our little Galileino, and in this coming period of Lent, when better times arrive, I will dearly love to see him again. I also yearn to share your belief that Vincenzio is all right, although I am not at all pleased with the way you come to this conclusion, namely without knowing anything for certain about him; but these are the fruits of a thankless world.

I am confounded to hear that you save my letters, and I suspect that the great love you bear me makes them seem more accomplished than they really are. But be that as it may, it is enough for me that you find satisfaction in them. With that I commend you to God, that He may be with you always, and I send you my usual loving greetings.   From San Matteo, the 18th of February 1630.

Sire's Most Affectionate Daughter,
Suor M. Celeste

Most Beloved Lord Father,
Because I am absolutely certain that by now you must have received my last letter, Sire, which I wrote many days ago, I will not repeat its content, except to assure you again of my well-being, and the good health of all my friends, by the grace of God. It is quite true that all these retreats and quarantines give, or rather have given, my imagination too much play, while they prevented me from receiving frequent news of you, Sire. However, I do believe that any day now they shall have to come to an end, and as a result we will soon be able to see you again. Meanwhile I want to know if you are well, because that is what matters to me above all else, and also if you have word of Vincenzio and my sister-in-law.

I am returning two empty flasks, and I send you these little spiced cakes which I think you will enjoy, being, as I suspect, cooked a bit longer than that other one, which your teeth may still recall.

The rainy weather of late has kept me from making you any of the rosemary flower jam, which I have been meaning to do, but the moment I am able to dry the flowers, I will prepare some and send it to you. For now I offer you loving greetings together with Suor Arcangela and the usual friends. I pray Our Lord to keep you in His holy grace, and I want you to give yet another kiss to little Galileino with my love.   From San Matteo, the 9th of March 1630.

Sire's Most Affectionate Daughter,
Suor M. Celeste

Most Illustrious and Beloved Lord Father,
Your letter brought me deep distress for many reasons, Sire, and primarily because it bears the news of Uncle Michelangelo's death, for which I feel so sorry, not only over the loss of him, but also anticipating the burden that consequently must fall on you, which I truly fear will not be the lightest to bear

among your other considerable worries, or, to say it better, tribulations. But, since blessed God lavishes upon you His gifts of long life and great ability, Sire, far more generously than He favored your brother or sisters, it is only fitting that you expend the one and bend the other to the absolute power of His Divine Majesty, who is our Master.

Thus if you had some expedient for Vincenzio, then, by his earning an income, your difficulties and expenses would be lightened, Sire, while at the same time his opportunities for complaining could be curtailed. Please, my lord father, since you were born and kept in this world for the benefit of so many, endeavor to put your own son first ahead of all these others; I speak of finding a means to ease his way. Because, as for the rest of your dealings with him, I know that no recommendations are needed, but on this particular matter I speak for your ears only, Sire, compelled by my own yearning to hear that you are at peace and joined in union with our Vincenzio and his wife, and that you all live together in tranquility. I have no doubt that this will come to pass, if you will do him this additional kindness, so strongly desired by him, as I know from the many times I have talked to him about it.

I am terribly disturbed by my inability to grant you satisfaction as I would have liked to do taking custody here of La Virginia, for whom I feel such fondness, considering all the sweet relief and diversion she has been to you, Sire. However I know that our superiors have declared themselves totally opposed to our admitting young girls, either as nuns or as charges, because the extreme poverty of our Convent, with which you are well acquainted, Sire, makes it a struggle to sustain those of us who are already here, let alone consider the addition of new mouths to feed. This being the most likely response, and also the general rule regarding relatives and outsiders, I could not dare to propose such a thing to Madonna or the other elders. Be assured that I suffer great anguish in disappointing you on this score, but in the end I see no alternative.

It also upsets me greatly to learn that you find yourself in poor health; and if I were allowed, how willingly I would take your burdens on my shoulders. But since that is impossible, I

shall not fail to pray, for you more than for myself. Thus may
it please the Lord to hear my prayer.

My health is good enough for me to observe Lent, with the
hope of seeing it through to the end, so that you must abandon
all thoughts of sending me any more treats for Carnival, Sire. I
thank you for those you have already sent, and to close I offer
you loving greetings with all my heart together with Suor Arcangela and our friends.   From San Matteo, the 11th of March
1630.

    Sire's Most Affectionate Daughter,
    Suor M. Celeste

If you have no one to whom you can give your leftover meat,
Sire, I will be very happy to distribute it, as the last you sent
was so appreciated. Thus, if you were to have the opportunity,
you could send me more of it sometime.

Most Beloved Lord Father,
I thank you, Sire, for your most welcome loving attention to us,
since this year of hardships causes us to pass the present Lenten
season so meagerly supplied, although, when one has one's
health, everything else is more easily tolerated.

We are all eagerly awaiting your arrival, Sire, along with little Galileo, just as soon as you can possibly come. Meanwhile
I cheer myself with the news that you are faring reasonably
well, even though I regret anew the obstacle that prevented me
from helping Virginia and pleasing you: I trust nonetheless that
blessed God will provide for her in some other manner.

If Vincenzio remains suspicious of your possible contagion,
Sire, that will be to your advantage, since no one takes money
from a person infected with the plague; and thus he, who has
such great fear of the disease, will demand no funds from you,
Sire, to whom I send my loving greetings. God bless you.
From San Matteo, the 12th of March 1630.

    Your Most Affectionate Daughter,
    Suor M. Celeste

Most Beloved Lord Father,
I no longer stand astonished by the extreme fervor of the affection you bear me, Sire, for you have given me too many signs and expressions of it; but I am indeed amazed that the love reaches so far beyond what I am capable of predicting, by your sending me a delicacy better suited to my taste and my health than any other Lenten food whatsoever. Therefore I thank you from the bottom of my heart, and I am prepared to enjoy it with doubled pleasure, knowing it was made by those hands I love and respect so much. And now that you order me to ask for another dish I like, I would request something for the evening meal, and as for the rest, please, Sire, put it out of your thoughts; because when I do have need of something, I will let it be known, confident that I can do so with complete security.

I cannot wait to see you again together with the baby, provided that it is not on a feast day because duties would prohibit us from welcoming you properly then.

I leave it to you to judge, Sire, whether the favor you intend to obtain from Monsignor Archbishop will console me; but I cannot resolve the matter just yet. I will spend some time with the Mother Abbess, and as soon as it becomes possible I shall let you know what I have been able to find out. Meanwhile I come to the end of this letter, without ever coming to the end of my loving regards for you. And I pray Our Lord to bless you. From San Matteo, the 13th of March 1630.

Your Most Affectionate Daughter,
SUOR M. CELESTE

Most Beloved Lord Father,
The response that I report from the Mother Abbess, regarding the service of which you wrote the other day, Sire, is that without doubt your procuring the favor from Monsignor Archbishop will be greatly and universally appreciated, not only by the fathers, but by the brothers as well [church governors and friars minor]; but that it seems most fitting to delay the request

until after Easter. Meanwhile, Sire, you will have been here and had the chance to speak of it directly with her, as she is truly a very judicious and discreet person, although quite timid.

I return your bleached collars which, for being so worn, cannot be done up with that perfection I would have wanted: if you need anything else remember that I have no greater pleasure in the world than busying myself taking care of whatever you would have me do, just as you, for your part, seem to have naught else to do but delight me and satisfy all my requests, since you provide for my every need with such solicitude.

I thank you for everything in general, and in particular for the most recent gifts that I received by hand from our steward, which were two little wrapped packets, one of almonds, the other of notebooks, and 6 *cantucci*. We enjoyed everything with thanks to you. And I have made you a poor man's present, namely this jar of conserve, which will be good for relieving your headache: although I think you might be better comforted by leaving off working yourself to exhaustion with study and writing. The trifles in the little basket are for our Virginia.

For want of time I will say no more. Except that in the name of all our friends I send you loving regards and pray Our Lord to grant you His holy grace.   From San Matteo, the 17th of March 1630.

> *Sire's Most Affectionate Daughter,*
> SUOR MARIA CELESTE

Most Beloved Lord Father,
The duties of the apothecary have kept me and still keep me so busy, that they prohibit me from saying anything else for now, if not that I acknowledge my involuntary delay and lateness in visiting with you by letter: now that I am allowed, I send to hear whether you feel well and if you have news of Vincenzio and my sister-in-law, namely if you think they will come to you this Most Holy Easter, which I think would thrill you, Sire, and me as well for loving you.

The cakes I send you are small ones; nevertheless I believe that they will suffice, now that you have no one to share them with except perhaps little Galileino, who will be able to amuse himself getting the nuts out of the pine cones we are sending him, which are all the ones the nun who tends our garden delivered here, to Suor Arcangela and me. I am not returning the little pot from the spinach because it is not completely empty; as the spinach is so tasty I am eating it slowly and sparingly. I greet you on behalf of all our usual friends, and I pray blessed God to keep you happy always.   From San Matteo, the 11th of April 1631.

Your Most Affectionate Daughter,
Suor M. Celeste

Most Beloved Lord Father,
If your letter had not assured me that your illness is of no great concern, I would certainly have felt even more upset than I do: and hearing that you are improving quickly, I hold on to the hope of soon seeing you again in perfect health, as you promise me.

We received via Vincenzio two dozen eggs and half a lamb, and we thank you, indeed, and even more so, for the four *piastre* [about three *scudi*] which arrive in a time of great monetary need.

La Piera is prepared to leave this instant, wherefore I reserve my writing for another day at greater length. Meanwhile I send you love with all my heart together with our usual friends. May Our Lord be with you always.   From San Matteo, the 22nd of April 1631.

Your Most Affectionate Daughter,
Suor M. Celeste

Most Illustrious and Beloved Lord Father,
Because I heard from La Piera the other day that you had
grown very listless again, Sire, and unable to eat anything, I
went in search of whatever I might be able to send you to help
you recover your appetite; and because I have heard the doctors recommend the Oxilacchara for this problem, I made a
small amount for you to experiment with, as it is something
that cannot do you any harm: the ingredients include nothing
but sugar, strong pomegranate wine, and a little vinegar. It is
very true that my preparation of it turned out a bit more con-
centrated than required, Sire, but you may take two or three
teaspoons of it in the morning, and to mitigate its bitterness,
add to it some cinnamon water, which, if you need more, I will
send to you, provided you return the vial I used the last time.

The little candies are from all the citrons you sent me, and I
believe they are very good; and if I knew of something else that
would prove to be to your liking, I would not fail to make
every effort to provide it, not only to please you, Sire, but also
myself; since serving you makes me extremely happy. I beseech
you, if you think of anything, to not deprive me of this contentment, and also to let me know how you feel now: with that,
praying Our Lord for your every benefit, I send you regards
with all my love together with our friends.   From San Matteo, the 25th of April 1631.

> *Sire's Most Affectionate Daughter,*
> SUOR M. CELESTE

Most Illustrious Lord Father,
As far as I have been able to determine, the priest of Monteri-
paldi has no jurisdiction over the villa of Signora Dianora
Landi save for a single field. I understand, however, that the
house was assigned as a dowry to a chapel of the Church of
Santa Maria del Fiore, and this is the reason that our same Signora Dianora finds herself in litigation. From the bearer of my

letter, who is a very shrewd woman with acquaintances all over Florence, you will be able to discover, Sire, who is contesting this case, since she knows the man, and then from him you can find out more information about the sale. [Here Galileo wrote in the margin, "This is Mr. Curzio Sportelli."]

I have also learned that Mannelli's villa is not yet taken, but is available for rent. This is a very beautiful property, and people say its air is the best in the whole region. I do not believe that you will lack the opportunity to secure it, Sire, if events turn out as well as you and I so strongly desire; and perhaps from this same woman you can receive some guidance.

I had accepted your vinegar for the oxymel because ours struck me as not being of the high quality I would have liked; now that you have been so kind as to send me the wine in exchange, Sire, I thank you for it and I am waiting to learn whether you are satisfied with the fruits of our labor, and when we will be allowed to do more for you, as this is the ardent wish of Suor Luisa and my other companions in the apothecary, all of whom, together with Suor Arcangela, send you their love. And I pray Our Lord for your every true happiness. From San Matteo, the 18th of May 1631.

Your Most Affectionate Daughter,
Suor Maria Celeste

Most Beloved Lord Father,
I have the utmost desire to enlist your aid, Sire, in giving a sign of gratitude and recognition for all my indebtedness to Suor Luisa, now that an appropriate occasion has arisen; since, as she finds herself in need of borrowing the sum of twenty-four *scudi* until the end of July, I would like to entreat you to do her this favor, if you could, as I imagine you can, Sire. And if it is true, as I know it to be absolutely true, that you want to give me every satisfaction and enjoyment, Sire, I assure you that this will be one of the greatest joys you could possibly provide me: and her nature is such that I do not doubt she will repay you

fully, most likely well before the end of the prescribed term of two months, as soon as she receives the guaranteed allowance from her income; for honestly, if matters stood otherwise, I would not even try to involve you in some imbroglio, as took place in the past to my everlasting regret. I will not dwell on this any longer, assuming that it would be superfluous to extend myself in lengthy entreaties to someone whose desire to shower me with goodness exceeds my own desire for any particular favor; I shall simply wait to be completely contented in this matter.

Meanwhile I tell you that I was extremely pleased that Monsignor Rinuccini was elected Archbishop, for your sake and ours, Sire, as we will discuss when the time is right.

I still do not know whether the first or the second oxymel I sent you was more to your liking, since you have not said anything about either: and because you have not yet sent the aloe and rhubarb for making your papal pills, here are two doses of ours, which you have taken previously, along with the promise to make you more of them whenever you like.

The citrons are most beautiful and both Suor Luisa and I will try to make the candies taste as good as the fruit looks, so that he who gave them will be only too happy to give us more of them in the future. Meanwhile I thank you very much for these, Sire, as well as for the glass jars, for which I am so grateful; and praying Our Lord for your every true blessing, I greet you lovingly along with my usual companions, and especially Suor Arcangela, who is feeling rather weak.   From San Matteo, the 23rd of May 1631.

Sire's Most Affectionate Daughter,
SUOR M. CELESTE

Most Illustrious and Beloved Lord Father,
Suor Luisa has enjoined me that I must, on her behalf, render to you those thanks she thinks I am better able to offer, for the comfort and attention she has received from you with such

promptness and courtesy; but as I know myself to be utterly
unfit for this task, I will pass over it in silence, persuaded as I
am that you will be happier knowing that I understand myself,
and confess myself indebted for an almost infinite multitude of
blessings conferred by you: and for this reason all my desire is
centered and focused solely upon not being ungrateful to you,
although indeed I cannot give you a better indication of gratitude than my good will; it is surely true that this last kindness
you have performed for me, Sire, to my mind, surpasses all the
previous ones, since you thus signify your devotion to my well-
being with expressions of generosity and love not only to me,
but also to those who command my devotion and obligation,
whereby I am doubly rewarded; and to my Suor Luisa I begin
to repay a debt that I can satisfy only with your help.

The candied citron morsels, since they turned out to be
among the most beautiful ones that I have ever made, must also
therefore taste the best; and I would not want you to give them
all away, Sire, even if you took pleasure in doing so: there are 8
of them.

As you know, Suor Arcangela continues the purging; and the
doctor deems it necessary to give her Tettuccio water [a diuretic
drawn from the Tettucio thermal spring near Pistoia], but in
small quantities, on account of her being feeble and sluggish;
and because this treatment requires very excellent care of the
body, and I find myself quite short of funds, I would dearly
hope that you could send me a couple of chickens, Sire, so I
could make broth for her both Friday and Saturday. Suor Chiara
is still sick in bed, so that with all of this and the duties of the
apothecary, I have sent idleness into exile, on the contrary I
would find myself overwhelmingly aggravated if Suor Luisa
were not willing, by her goodness, to share in all my labors. I
send you greetings from her and Suor Arcangela, and I pray
blessed God to grant you long life for your sake and mine.
From San Matteo, the 4th of June 1631.

Sire's Most Affectionate Daughter,
SUOR M. CELESTE

Most Beloved Lord Father,
Sunday morning brought Vincenzio here, telling me he had come to see the Perini villa, as I recall, which is for sale, and, as far as I understand, the buyer will have every advantage, as you will no doubt be informed, Sire, by Vincenzio himself. For my part, because I hear that it is very close to us, and because I prize your satisfaction, Sire (knowing how much you want to be near us), along with that of Vincenzio and ours as well, I come to beg you not to let this opportunity slip through your fingers, for God knows when another such as this will present itself, now that we see how people who own properties in these parts cling to them, except in extreme necessity, as is now the case with these people and also Mannelli, whose villa I hear may have already been rented. If you decide to come and look yourself at this other one, you will be able to use the occasion to visit us as well. Meanwhile I assure you that I am fine, but not so Suor Arcangela, who is at last confined to bed: her illness is not one of grave concern, but I sincerely believe that, if she were not thus provided for, she would incur some far more serious malady. I received the hens for her and I thank you a thousandfold. I pray our Lord to bless you, and I send you regards with all my love, together with our usual friends.   From San Matteo, the 10th of June 1631.
> *Sire's Most Affectionate Daughter,*
> Suor M. Celeste

Most Beloved Lord Father,
Suor Luisa has by good fortune collected her income ahead of schedule, and she comes immediately to make good the loan of the 24 *scudi* that she owes you, Sire. She readily confesses being neither willing nor able to satisfy that other obligation she will always bear you, as her spirit is not appeased by offering only money in exchange for all your kindness and tenderness, but also seeks to repay you in the currency of a true and cordial affection for you as well as for us; and this she manifests daily

by helping me in every contingency, in such a way that she could not do more for me if she were my own mother. She has added to the basket these little cakes, Sire, for you to enjoy with her love.

Suor Arcangela is in bed with a very slight fever, but great weakness and many pains, and, if I am not mistaken, I believe there will be much to do before she recovers her health, if she ever does. The doctor, when he last visited her, ordered among other things several stomach ointments made with stomach oil from the Grand Duke, and oil of nutmeg. We have neither of these, Sire, and therefore I would be most appreciative if you could get me some.

I am returning two empty flasks, and truly, in this slump I have had, were it not for your white wine, Sire, things would have gone much worse, since I sustain myself on pap and soup, which have not hurt me for being made with such good wine.

I will be eager to hear if you settle the purchase of the villa you came to see, Sire, because I want that so much: and the arrangement would seem to me a very good and helpful one for that household. Not having anything else to say at present, I send you loving greetings together with the others here, and I pray blessed God to keep you happy always.   From San Matteo, the [blank] day of July 1631.

Sire's Most Affectionate Daughter,
SUOR M. CELESTE

Most Illustrious and Beloved Lord Father,
Because I do so desire the grace of your moving closer to us, Sire, I am continually trying to learn when places here in our vicinity are to be let. And now I hear anew of the availability of the villa of Signor Esaù Martellini, which lies on the Piano dei Giullari, and adjacent to us. I wanted to call it to your attention, Sire, so that you could make inquiries to see if by chance it might suit you, which I would love, hoping that with this proximity I would not be so deprived of news of you, as happens to me now, this being a situation I tolerate most unwill-

ingly; but taking it into account and accepting it along with a few other trifling aversions, as opposed to those mortifications which I omit out of negligence, I bend myself as best I can to God's will. Beyond that I am convinced that you, too, Sire, do not lack for intrigues and troubles of an altogether different stamp from mine, and this silences me.

Suor Arcangela, who has preoccupied my thoughts, by the grace of God fares somewhat better, and although she still finds herself quite weak and listless, she is starting to sit up. And since she seems to have a taste for some salted fish, I entreat you, Sire, to try to provide her with some for these next fasting days. Meanwhile you must endeavor to keep yourself healthy in this terrible heat, and please write me a line. I send you loving greetings from all of us here, and I pray Our Lord to grant you His holy grace.   From San Mattteo, the 12th of August 1631.

Sire's Most Affectionate Daughter,
SUOR M. CELESTE

Most Beloved Lord Father,
We lament the time away from you, Sire, covetous of the pleasure we would have drawn from this day, had we found ourselves all together in each other's company. But, if it please God, I expect that this will soon come to pass, and in the meanwhile I enjoy the hope of having you here always near us, as I understand from the message given me by La Piera; and I pray you to persist in this enterprise so that it succeeds according to our plan, because, if you will it so, Sire, I believe you can overcome every difficulty.

This evening I will share the bounty you sent me with my friends, but I will not promise them too much of the ricotta; I thank you on their behalf and I give you the loving greetings of my heart.   From San Matteo, the 27th of August 1631.

Your Most Affectionate Daughter,
SUOR M. CELESTE

Most Beloved Lord Father,
If the measure or indication of the love one bears another person is the trust vested in the loved one, then you must never doubt, Sire, that I love you with all my heart, as in truth I do; since I draw such confidence and security from you that at times I fear I exceed the bounds of modesty and filial devotion, and all the more so as I know you to be beset by many worries and expenses. Nevertheless the certainty I have, that you will minister ever so much more willingly to my needs than to those of any other person, even including your own, lets me dare to ask you if you would be so kind as to relieve me of a worry that weighs heavily on my mind, regarding a debt I owe of five *scudi* incurred during Suor Arcangela's illness, as I was constrained during these four months to spend with largesse, compared to the economy that befits the poverty of our station: and now that I find myself desperate and pressed to repay the loan, I come to the one I know is willing and able to help me. And also I want a *fiasco* of your white wine to make a strengthening tonic for Suor Arcangela, who I think will be better served by her faith in this remedy than by the remedy itself.

I write with so little time that I cannot possibly say more, except that I hope you enjoy these six almond pastries, and I send you my love.   From San Matteo, the 30th of August 1631.
Your Most Affectionate Daughter,
SUOR M. CELESTE

[In September, Galileo moves into a house around the corner from the convent. Suor Maria Celeste's next letter, eighteen months later, marks his departure for Rome to stand trial.]

Most Illustrious and Beloved Lord Father,
The Bocchineri family have managed to bring me all the letters that you sent, Sire, and from their number I feel certain I know how tired you must be of writing. I have not written to you un-

til now, because I was waiting to hear word of your arrival in Rome; and having learned from this last letter of yours that you are required to spend so many days in such poor lodgings [detained in quarantine in Acquapendente because of the plague in Florence], deprived of every comfort, I am extremely distressed. Nevertheless, hearing that while you lack all internal and external consolations, you still maintain your health, I console myself and give thanks to blessed God, steadfastly confident that by His grace you will return to us, Sire, with peace of mind and soundness of body. Meanwhile I entreat you to be as cheerful as you possibly can, and commend yourself to God, as He does not abandon those who put their trust in Him.

Suor Arcangela and I are well, but I cannot say as much for Suor Luisa, who, since the day of your departure has been confined to bed with the same terrible pains that have stricken her in the past; and I am content to stay continually active and take charge of applying her treatments and waiting on her, as this emergency relieves my mind of dwelling too disturbingly on your absence.

Signor Rondinelli [the Grand Duke's librarian] has not yet arrived to enjoy the convenience you so graciously granted him of using your house, Sire, explaining that his litigations have prevented him. But our father confessor has gone there often to look it over; he sends his regards to you, and so do the Mother Abbess and all our friends; Suor Arcangela and I with all our hearts and without ceasing pray Our Lord constantly to protect you and bless you.

This enclosure I am sending you was found Monday by Giuseppe [Galileo's servant boy] in the place where your letters are usually delivered.   From San Matteo, the 5th of February 1632.

Sire's Most Affectionate Daughter,
Suor M. Celeste

Most Illustrious and Beloved Lord Father,
Your letter written on the 10th of February was delivered to me
on the 22nd of the same month, and by now I assume you must
have received another letter of mine, Sire, along with one from
our father confessor, and through these you will have learned
some of the details you wanted to know; and seeing that still no
letters have come giving us definite news of your arrival in
Rome (and you can imagine, Sire, with what eagerness I in particular anticipate those letters), I return to write to you again,
so that you may know how anxiously I live, while awaiting
word from you, and also to send you the enclosed legal notice,
which was delivered to your house, 4 or 5 days ago, by a young
man, and accepted by Signor Francesco Rondinelli, who, in
giving it to me, advised me that it must be paid, without waiting for some more offensive insult from the creditor, telling me
that one could not disobey such an order in any manner, and
offering to handle the matter himself. This morning I gave him
the 6 *scudi,* which he did not want to pay to Vincenzio [Lan-
ducci, her cousin] but chose to deposit the money with the
magistrate until you have told him, Sire, what you want him to
do. Signor Francesco is indeed a most pleasant and discreet
person, and he never stops declaiming his gratefulness to you,
Sire, for allowing him the use of your house. I heard from La
Piera that he treats her and Giuseppe with great kindness, even
in regard to their foods; and I provide for the rest of their
needs, Sire, according to your directions. The boy tells me that
this Easter he will need shoes and stockings, which I plan to
knit for him out of thick, coarse cotton or else from fine wool.
La Piera maintains that you have often spoken to her about or-
dering a bale of linen, on which account I refrained from buying the small amount I would need to begin weaving the thick
cloth for your kitchen, as I had meant to do, Sire, and I will not
make the purchase unless I hear otherwise from you.

The vines in the garden will take nicely now that the Moon
is right, at the hands of Giuseppe's father, who they say is capable enough, and also Signor Rondinelli will lend his help.
The lettuce I hear is quite lovely, and I have entrusted Giuseppe

to take it to be sold at market before it spoils. From the sale of 70 bitter oranges came 4 *lire,* a very respectable price, from what I understand, as that fruit has few uses: Portuguese oranges are selling for 14 *crazie* per 100 and you had 200 that were sold.

As for that barrel of newly tapped wine you left, Sire, Signor Rondinelli takes a little for himself every evening, and meanwhile he makes improvements to the wine, which he says is coming along extremely well. What little of the old wine that was left I had decanted into flasks, and told La Piera that she and Giuseppe could drink it when they had finished their small cask, since we of late have had reasonably good wine from the convent, and, being in good health, have hardly taken a drop.

I continue to give one *giulio* [about half a *lira*] every Saturday to La Brigida, and I truly consider this an act of charity well deserved, as she is so exceedingly needy and such a very good girl.

Suor Luisa, God bless her, fares somewhat better, and is still purging, and having understood from your last letter, Sire, how concerned you were over her illness out of your regard for her, she thanks you with all her heart; and while you declare yourself united with me in loving her, Sire, she on the other hand claims to be the paragon of this emotion, nor do I mind granting her that honor, since her affection stems from the same source as yours, and it is myself; wherefore I take pride in and prize this most delicious contest of love, and the more clearly I perceive the greatness of that love you both bear me, the more bountiful it grows for being mutually exchanged between the very two persons I love and revere above everyone and everything in this life.

Tomorrow will be 15 days since the death of our Suor Virginia Canigiani, who was already gravely ill when I last wrote to you, Sire, and since then a malevolent fever has stricken Suor Maria Grazia del Pace, the eldest of the three nuns who play the organ, and teacher of the Squarcialupis, a truly tranquil and good nun; and since the doctor has already given her up for dead, we are all beside ourselves, grieving over our loss.

This is everything I need to tell you for the moment, and as soon as I receive your letters (which must surely have arrived at Pisa by now where the Bocchineri gentlemen are) I will write again. Meanwhile I send you the greetings of my heart together with our usual friends, and particularly Suor Arcangela, Signor Rondinelli and Doctor Ronconi, who begs me for news of you every time he comes here. May the Lord God bless you and keep you happy always.   From San Matteo, the 26th of February 1633.

> *Sire's Most Affectionate Daughter,*
> SUOR M. CELESTE GALILEI

Signor Rondinelli, having this very moment returned from Florence, tells me he spoke to the Chancellor of the Advisors and learned that the 6 *scudi* must be paid to Vincenzio Landucci and not be deposited, and this will be done; I submitted to this decision reluctantly, not having had your instructions on the matter.

Most Beloved Lord Father,
Signor Mario Guiducci [a former student of Galileo's, now an official with the Florentine Magistracy of Public Health] yesterday morning sent me, by one of his servants, all the way up here, the letters he had received from you. I read with especial delight the one you wrote to Signor Mario himself, and I sent it back to him right away. The other I gave to the Father Confessor, who I am certain will send a reply. I take comfort, and ever again I thank blessed God, hearing that your affairs thus far proceed with such tranquillity and silence, which bodes well for a happy and prosperous outcome, as I have always hoped would come with divine help and by the intercession of the most holy Blessed Virgin.

I believe that by now you will have received my last letter, Sire, and since then new tidings are the disbursement of the 6 *scudi* by Signor Francesco in your name to Vincenzio Landucci, who came in person to collect them; the good progress in recovery being achieved by Suor Luisa, she having been free of

pain for several days now; Suor Arcangela's illness of the past
ten days, which afflicts her with terrible soreness in her left
shoulder and arm, even though, with the help of various pills
and enemas, the symptoms are somewhat mitigated: and even
Giuseppe suffers from his stomach and swollen spleen, so that
he is constrained to break Lent, and Signor Rondinelli is taking
special care of him. More than that our Suor Maria Grazia, the
organist who had been gravely ill, as I notified you, Sire, has
died, at the age of 58 or 60 years, and all of us have felt grievously distressed. La Piera is well, the vines in the garden are
staked; the sale of lettuce to date has brought in half a *scudo*.

Other details I have none to tell you, except that all day long
I perform the office of Martha [patron saint of cooks and
housekeepers], without a single intermission, and thus I stay in
reasonably good health, which condition I would most willingly share with you, Sire, or rather exchange my well-being
for your indisposition, so that you could remain free of those
ills that molest you. I am waiting for the order regarding other
payments to the Landuccis for the present month, because I
would not want to make any mistakes, nor have us incur expenses as we did this time in the *lire* amounts of 6. 13. 4. which
appear on the bill I sent you. The letter to her ladyship the Ambassadress can be sealed after you have read it. And ending
here I give you all my loving greetings together with our usual
friends.   From San Matteo, the 5th of March 1632.

Your Most Affectionate Daughter,
S. M. Celes[. .]

Most Illustrious and Beloved Lord Father,
Your last letter, sent me from Signor Andrea Arrighetti [Galileo's
friend and fellow mathematician], brought me great solace, as
much for hearing that you are keeping up your good health,
Sire, as for the good news that assures me of a happy ending to
your affair, just as my longing and my love have led me to expect. Whereby even though I see that, with things progressing
in this fashion, prolonging the time of your return, I consider it

nonetheless a great destiny to be deprived of my own satisfaction for an occasion that has the potential to redound in the favorable recognition and reputation of your character, which I love more than my own. And I calm myself all the more by my certainty that you will receive every honor and desired comfort from those very excellent lords, and especially from my most excellent lady and patroness, whose visit, should Suor Arcangela and I be so fortunate as to receive one, would certainly be a noteworthy honor and as welcome to us as you will have to imagine yourself, Sire, for I know not how to express it. [Ambassador Francesco Niccolini and his wife, Caterina, are Galileo's hosts at the Tuscan Embassy in Rome.] As for allowing her to view a play, I am speechless, because it would have to be rehearsed in time for her arrival, while I honestly believe, since she has evinced this desire to hear us perform, Sire, that we would be safer leaving her believing in the talent she assumes us to have on your say-so. Similarly the arrival of the most reverend father Don Benedetto [Castelli, a Benedictine monk and one of Galileo's oldest friends and colleagues] will be most appreciated here, on account of his being a renowned individual and so affectionate toward you, Sire, so please return his regards twofold from us, and also do me the favor of giving me some news of Anna Maria [Vajani, a painter of floral themes], whom you extolled so highly the last time you returned from Rome, because since then I find myself growing attached to her, having heard of her goodness and courage.

Suor Arcangela feels somewhat improved, but her arm is not altogether better yet, and Suor Luisa fares reasonably well, by virtue of her strict observance of her daily regimen. I feel all right because my mind is calm and clear, while my body stays in constant motion, except for the seven hours of the night, which I waste away by only sleeping, because this dull head of mine cannot survive with even a tiny bit less. I do not fail in any case to devote as much time as possible to my prayers, entreating blessed God to grant you first of all the health of your soul, and also the other favors that you most desire.

I will say no more for now, if not to beg your forbearance if I have bored you too much, thinking that I could compress into this paper all the things I would chatter to you about in a week's time. I send you all my love together with our usual friends; and Signor Rondinelli sends you his regards.   From San Matteo, the 12th of March 1632.

Sire's Most Affectionate Daughter,
SUOR M. CELESTE

Most Illustrious and Beloved Lord Father,
Signor Mario [Guiducci], with his usual kindness, sent me your letters yesterday morning. I have forwarded the two enclosed ones to their intended recipients; and I thank you for your advice about the error I had committed in my letter to her ladyship the Ambassadress, from whom I have the most courteous letter in response to mine; and among other things she tells me that she encourages you, Sire, to come and go with greater freedom in their house, indeed with the same assurance as you would enter your own, and she shows herself very concerned about your comfort and satisfaction. I am writing to them again to ask her for a favor that you will see, Sire: if it seems proper to propose this to her, I will be only too happy to do so; if not, I will conform to your wish. But truly, whether by the help of her ladyship the Ambassadress, or from you, Sire, I would dearly love to obtain this good will, since I would like to have a gift from you upon your return, which event I surely hope will not have to be delayed much longer. I imagine there must be an abundance of good artwork available where you are, and so I would like you to bring me a small picture, about the size of the enclosed paper, in the form of a diptych that would stand open like a little prayerbook, with two figures, one of which I should want to be an Ecce Homo [Jesus crucified] and the other a Madonna; but I would want each to be executed as piously and devoutly as possible. There is no need for any adornment other than a simple frame, as I intend to keep this always near me.

I believe without doubt that Signor Rondinelli must be writing to you, Sire, wherefore you would do well in your response to acknowledge the thoughtfulness he has shown us from time to time during this season of Lent, and especially because yesterday he was here to dine and he wished the two of us to join him, so that we might pass the halfway point of Lent happily, mostly for love of Suor Arcangela, who by the grace of God is finding her arm improved. The fact is, Sire, with Suor Oretta having been stricken several days ago by a catarrh in the small of her back, and thus unable to exert herself, I have had to assume most of the responsibilities of the Provider's office, and between this and my other duties, I am reduced to writing at midnight and assailing my sleep, so that I fear I may say something inappropriate. I take delight, however, in hearing that you guard your health, Sire, and I pray blessed God to keep you well. I send you regards from all our friends and also in the name of Doctor Ronconi, who often asks after you with great concern.   From San Matteo, the 19th of March 1632.

Sire's Most Affectionate Daughter,
SUOR M. CELESTE

Most Illustrious and Beloved Lord Father,
You have wanted me to remain mortified through these holy days, Sire, depriving me of your letters, which, as much as I have felt about it, I cannot express in words. But still I do not want to neglect, despite the severe constraints on my time, to greet you with these two lines, wishing you joyfully a most holy Easter, replete with spiritual consolations and good health and temporal happiness, for all that I promise myself for you and hope from the most generous hand of the Lord God.

Here for the present, God be praised, we are all well, but not so our Giuseppe, who, after the holidays, will need to go to the hospital to have his fever treated, and see to his spleen, which is greatly distended; wherefore I am trying, with the help of our Mother Abbess, to have him received in Bonifazio [the city hospital in Florence], where he will be better cared for than anywhere else. La Piera fares well and sends you her regards, as do I with all my heart together with our usual friends, and I remind you that you now owe me responses to three letters. From San Matteo, Holy Saturday 1633.

Sire's Most Affectionate Daughter,
SUOR M. CELESTE

Most Illustrious and Beloved Lord Father,
Last Saturday I saw the letter you wrote to Signor Andrea Arrighetti, Sire, and it gave me especial pleasure to hear that you are not only keeping yourself well, but rather gaining something with the help of that peace of mind you enjoy, while you hope for a placid and rapid settlement of your affair; for all of this may blessed God be ever praised, as He is the principal source of these graces.

I also had a great desire to know, Sire, if you gave my letter to Her Ladyship the Ambassadress, and if so whether it may have been improper, as I feared, to ask her that favor [procuring the diptych of Jesus and Mary], which with her help I hope to secure, as her incomparable courtesy assures me she will employ every diligence to obtain it. I want you to help me, Sire, by making the required ceremonial gestures for me; and beyond this I have another kindness to ask of you, not for myself, but for Suor Arcangela, who, by the grace of God, three weeks from today, which will be the last day of this month, must leave the office of Provider [her term as manager of outside food purchases], in which capacity up till now she has spent one hundred *scudi* and fallen into debt; and being obliged to leave 25 *scudi* in reserve for the new Provider, not having anywhere else to turn, I beg your leave, with your permission, Sire, to help her out with the money of yours that I hold, so that this ship can bring itself safely to port, whereas truly, without your help, it would not complete so much as half its voyage. But there is no need for me to exhaust myself in exaggerating this situation, when it can all be explained by saying that every good thing we have, and we do have so much, or all that we may hope and desire, we have and we hope from you, Sire, from your extraordinary loving kindness and charity, with which, beyond having politely met your obligation as a parent to provide for us, you continuously assist us so graciously in all our needs: but you see, Sire, how blessed God rewards you on our behalf, as He deigns to grant you continued health and prosperity, keeping you and us happy all this time.

The excessive pain in my tooth keeps me from being able to write at length, so that I will not give you other news, except that Giuseppe is getting better, and all of us are well: together with La Piera and everyone here we send you our loving regards. From San Matteo, the 9th of April 1633.

Sire's Most Affectionate Daughter,
SUOR M. CELESTE

Most Beloved Lord Father,
Two letters from you this week inform me of the good progress of your affair: in this I rejoice as much as you can possibly imagine, Sire, and I thank God for it.

Yesterday evening here there was a great outburst of cheer and merriment, celebrating the successful intercession of Her Most Excellent Ladyship the Ambassadress, to whom I write the few lines enclosed herewith, which barely begin to thank her for all the many blessings I draw from her. I do as much as I can, though not nearly as much as I think I should. I wrote to Sig. Giovanni Rinuccini to request a bill for his services, as you asked me to do, Sire, and he answered that for now there is no need to speak of this business, but that, when the time comes, he will advise me.

I understand there are several cases of the evil pestilence in Florence, but not nearly as many as reports where you are would have you believe. I hear that there are buboes, but that more people die of rashes and lung disease. As for how this affects your return, as urgently as I desire it, I would advise you to leave it imminent for a while yet, awaiting other advice from your friends, and also to carry out the idea you had when you left here, of visiting the House of the Virgin Mary in Loreto.

Our Vincenzio wrote to us this week, and sent us as a gift a piece of ham; I would be curious to know how often he visits you, Sire, with his letters. Giuseppe is so greatly improved that he has left the hospital, and is staying for several days at the home of his uncle in Florence. La Piera fares well and tends to her spinning. She picked a few small lemons that were hanging from the low branches, before they could be carried off by thieves. The rest I hear are coming along very beautifully, and the same may be said for the broad beans, which are beginning to produce a great yield. How I hope that you will be back in your garden to pick them yourself, Sire, when they are perfectly ripe.

I send you loving greetings on behalf of everyone here, as well as from their Lordships Rondinelli and Orsi; and from the Lord God I pray for every genuine goodness to be yours. From San Matteo, the 16th of April 1633.

> *Your Most Affectionate Daughter,*
> SUOR M. CELESTE

Our Suor Isabella wants you to do her the favor, Sire, of having your servant hand-deliver the enclosed letter to its addressee, because she would like an immediate response.

Our chaplain, who came to give the blessed water, asked after you the moment he arrived, Sire, urging me to pay you his respects.

Most Beloved Lord Father,
I did not have time this morning to be able to respond fully to your offer, which was that you intended to give comfort and come to the aid of just us two, and not the whole convent, as per chance you persuade yourself may be the case, Sire, when you help settle the debt for Suor Arcangela's office. I see verily that you are not entirely informed of our customs, or, to say it

more correctly, our indiscreet system of unofficial rules; for, as each one of us is compelled by turns to assume the expenditures of the Provider's office, and of all the other convent offices, it is incumbent upon every nun, as the various responsibilities devolve upon her, to find the requisite sum of money to meet the particular need in each case, and if she does not have it, the worse for her; wherefore many times it happens that by indirect and roundabout means (this I have learned from you, Sire) these sisters find ways to provide the required services by embroiling themselves in many predicaments: and it is impossible for them to manage it otherwise, when any poor nun in the office of Provider must spend one hundred *scudi*. For Suor Arcangela up till now I have paid close to 40, part of which I had received as a loan from Suor Luisa, and part from our allowance, of which there remains a balance of 16 *scudi* to draw upon for all of May. Suor Oretta spent 50 *scudi*: Now we are sorely pressed and I do not know where else to turn, and since the Lord God keeps you in this life for our support, I take advantage of this blessing and seize upon it to beseech you, Sire, that with God's love you free me from the worry that harasses me, by lending me whatever amount of money you can until next year comes around, at which time we will recover our losses by collecting from those who must pay the expenses then, and thereby repay you, with which thought, in haste, I commend you to God. [On the back of this letter, Galileo wrote, "Suor Maria Celeste needs money immediately."]

Your Most Affectionate Daughter,
Suor M. Celeste

Most Beloved Lord Father,
Signor Geri [Bocchineri—Sestilia's brother and secretary to the grand duke] informed me of the conditions imposed on you on account of your affair, Sire, that alas you are detained in the chambers of the Holy Office; on the one hand this gives me great distress, convinced as I am that you find yourself with

scant peace of mind, and perhaps also deprived of all bodily comforts: on the other hand, considering the need for events to reach this stage, in order for the authorities to dismiss you, as well as the kindliness with which everyone there has treated you up till now, and above all the justice of the cause and your innocence in this instance, I console myself and cling to the expectation of a happy and prosperous triumph, with the help of blessed God, to Whom my heart never ceases to cry out, commending you with all the love and trust it contains. [After months of waiting, Galileo gave his first deposition before the Inquisition on April 12.]

The only thing for you to do now is to guard your good spirits, taking care not to jeopardize your health with excessive worry, but to direct your thoughts and hopes to God, Who, like a tender, loving father, never abandons those who confide in Him and appeal to Him for help in time of need. Dearest lord father, I wanted to write to you now, to tell you I partake in your torments, so as to make them lighter for you to bear: I have given no hint of these difficulties to anyone else, wanting to keep the unpleasant news to myself, and to speak to the others only of your pleasures and satisfactions. Thus we are all awaiting your return, eager to enjoy your conversation again with delight. And who knows, Sire, if while I sit writing, you may not already find yourself released from your predicament and free of all concerns? Thus may it please the Lord, Who must be the One to console you, and in Whose care I leave you. From San Matteo, the 20th of April 1633.

Sire's Most Affectionate Daughter,
SUOR M. CELESTE

Most Illustrious and Beloved Lord Father,
Although in your last letter, Sire, you did not write me a single detail about your affair, perhaps to avoid making me a participant in your troubles, I, for my part, learned something, as you will be able to understand from my letter of last Wednesday.

And truly I have passed these past few days with my mind greatly distressed and perplexed until, receiving this letter of yours, I am assured of your well-being, and with this comfort I can breathe again. Nor will I neglect to carry out all that you have ordered me to do, thanking you meanwhile for the assurance of money that you make to Suor Arcangela, on behalf of us both, since all her worries are also mine.

Here in the Monastery everyone is healthy, thank God, but we hear much talk of the evil pestilence in Florence and also outside the city in several locations. And for this reason, please, even if you were to be released immediately, do not set out on your return journey in the face of such a manifest threat to your life, especially when the limitless kindness of those gentle people serving as your hosts will surely extend to letting you stay with them as long as you have need to.

Suor Luisa, together with the others you mentioned by name, all return your greetings twice over, and I pray the Lord God to bless you with the fullness of His grace. I ask you to pay my respects to Her Excellency, My Ladyship.   From San Matteo, the 23rd of April 1633.

Sire's Most Affectionate Daughter,
S. M. CELESTE

Most Beloved Lord Father,
I saw the last letter you wrote to Signor Geri, Sire, which truly is pure politeness and very solicitous in giving all the news of you; and, if indeed when you wrote it you found yourself indisposed, I hope that now you are well again, wherefore I calm myself, rejoicing to hear that your affair is headed on the right path toward a good outcome and a swift dispatch. This week I have had letters from Her Excellent Ladyship the Ambassadress, who with her usual courtesy had the kindness to inform me of your circumstances, Sire, for, as she tells me, she does not believe I have had any letters from you since you left her house, and she knows you want to keep my mind at ease; and this

gives me the clearest indication of the love these noble people feel for you, Sire, which is so abundant that it more than suffices to enfold me as well, as her Ladyship pledged to me most certainly in her ever so thoughtful letter. I have written back to them herewith, directing my letter to you, which seems the most appropriate thing to do.

There is good news regarding the plague, and we are hopeful, given what people say, that it will soon disappear altogether, and then, if it please God, you will not have this impediment preventing your return.

I am busy with the mason who is helping us, or, more precisely, is building for us a small stove for distilling, and on this account I must be brief. We are all feeling fine, except Suor Luisa, who for the past three days has been suffering on account of her stomach, although not as severely as at other times. Giuseppe fares reasonably well, and La Piera is fine. Signor Rondinelli sends you his regards and will do us the favor of paying the rent money to Signor Lorenzo Bini. The Father Confessor also sends you his good wishes, as do all of these nuns and Suor Arcangela most of all. May Our Lord bless you. From San Matteo, the last of April 1633.

Sire's Most Affectionate Daughter,
SUOR M. CELESTE

Most Illustrious and Beloved Lord Father,
The delight delivered to me by your latest loving letter was so great, and the change it wrought in me so extensive, that, taking the impact of the emotion together with my being compelled many times to read and reread the same letter over and over to these nuns, until everyone could rejoice in the news of your triumphant successes, I was seized by a terrible headache that lasted from the fourteenth hour of the morning on into the night, something truly outside my usual experience. [Galileo, having returned to the Tuscan Embassy after a second hearing in the chambers of the Holy Office, believes he has struck a deal with the Inquisitors that will help everyone save face.] I

wanted to tell you this detail, not to reproach you for my small suffering, but to enable you to understand all the more how heavily your affairs weigh on my heart and fill me with concern, by showing you what effects they produce in me; effects which, although, generally speaking, filial devotion can and should produce in all progeny, yet in me, I will dare to boast that they possess greater force, as does the power that places me far ahead of most other daughters in the love and reverence I bear my dearest Father, when I see clearly that he, for his part, surpasses the majority of fathers in loving me as his daughter: and that is all I have to say.

I offer endless thanks to blessed God for all the favors and graces that you have been granted up till now, Sire, and hope to receive in the future, since most of them issue from that merciful hand, as you most justly recognize. And even though you attribute the great share of these blessings to the merit of my prayers, this truly is little or nothing; what matters most is the sentiment with which I speak of you to His Divine Majesty, Who, respecting that love, rewarding you so beneficently, answers my prayers, and renders us ever more greatly obligated to Him, while we are also deeply indebted to all those people who have given you their goodwill and aid, and especially to those most preeminent nobles who are your hosts. And I did want to write to Her Most Excellent Ladyship the Ambassadress, but I stay my hand lest I vex her with my constant repetition of the same statements, these being expressions of thanks and confessions of my infinite indebtedness. You take my place, Sire, and pay respects to her in my name. And truly, dearest lord Father, the blessing that you have enjoyed from the favors and the protection of these dignitaries is so great that it suffices to assuage, or even annul all the aggravations you have endured.

Here is a copy I made you of a most excellent prescription against the plague that has fallen into my hands, not because I believe there is any suspicion of the malady where you are, but because this remedy also works well for all manner of ills. [The "prescription" has been lost, but apparently called for faith and virtue.] As to the ingredients, I am in such short supply that I must beg them for myself, on which account I cannot fill the prescription for anyone else; but you must try to procure those ingredients that perchance you may lack, Sire, from the heavenly foundry, from the depths of the compassion of the Lord God, with Whom I leave you. Closing with regards to you from everyone here, and in particular from Suor Arcangela and Suor Luisa, who for now, as far as her health is concerned, is getting along passing well.   From San Matteo, the 7th of May 1633.

Sire's Most Affectionate Daughter,
SUOR M. CELESTE

Most Beloved Lord Father,
That the letter you wrote me last week brought me the greatest pleasure and joy, I have already indicated to you in a previous note of mine; and now I add that being compelled to send it to Signor Geri so that Vincenzio too could see it, I made a copy, which Signor Rondinelli, after having read it, wanted to take with him to Florence, to spread the news among several friends of his, whom he knew would derive great satisfaction from hearing these particulars about you, Sire, as indeed turned out to be the case, for so I was informed later on when Signor Rondinelli returned the letter to me. He is the one who from time to time comes to your house, Sire, and no others frequent it. La Piera tells me she does not go out at all, except when she comes here, to hear mass or for other needs, and the boy sometimes goes as far as the Bocchineris' house to pick up the letters, not daring to venture elsewhere, because, beyond shunning anyone suspected of plague, he is still a weakling and moreover covered with mange he acquired in the hospital; and now he needs to medicate the rash with some ointment that I am making for him. As for the rest I attempt to tend to everything in the manner you will be able to see, Sire, in this scribbled account that I am sending you, where thus far I have noted the expenditures paid out, and also the income gained on account. The income, although it exceeds the expenses by several *lire,* I took the liberty of spending on necessities for Suor Arcangela and myself, so that you could say the accounts are balanced

now, and from this day forward I will make a new ledger. The other outlays after your departure, Sire, are,

Scudi 17 and a half to Signor Lorenzo Bini for the rent of the villa.

Scudi 24 in four payments to Vincenzio Landucci, and *lire 6. 13. 4* in expenses for February; and I have receipts for all of these.

Scudi 25 appropriated by me to care for Suor Arcangela, as you know, Sire, and others.

Scudi 15 it was necessary to take, so that she could finish her blessed office, which was conducted with the help of God and of you Sire, because, without this enormous relief, it would not have been possible to carry on; and also the nuns showed themselves entirely satisfied, because, with your loving attention, Sire, and your having provided money, they have covered up more bad deeds or secret vices than we wish to admit. These last 15 *scudi* I expect to repay you presently from our allowance, which we shall soon have to withdraw.

This current year was to bring Suor Arcangela's turn as Cellarer [in charge of the convent's wine cellar], an office that gave me much to ponder. Indeed I secured the Mother Abbess's pardon that it not be given to her by pleading various excuses; and instead she was made Draper, obliging her to bleach and keep count of the tablecloths and towels in the convent.

I feel particularly delighted to hear that your health is in good condition, Sire, as I was very worried about your well-being on account of the travails you have endured; but the Lord God wanted to grant you the combined graces of freeing you not only from the torments of the spirit but also those of the body. May He be ever praised!

The evil contagion still persists, but they say that only a few people die of it and the hope is that it must come to an end when the Madonna of Impruneta is carried in procession to Florence for this purpose. [This holy icon is carried in procession from Impruneta to Florence whenever disaster—flood, famine, war— threatens the city.]

I sent your letter to our former Father Confessor in Florence, since he no longer comes to our convent, and we have had another confessor, a young man of 35 years, from the parish church of San Stefano.

I am stupefied to learn that Vincenzio has never written to you, and I revel in having outstripped him by my zeal in visiting you with my letters, although frequently I too had great strictures on my time, and today I have written this one in four installments, interrupted constantly by various complications for the sake of the apothecary; and further by toothache that brings on my typical catarrh, which has already troubled me for several days.

I end by greeting you on behalf of everyone mentioned herein, and entreating you to return the regards of my Most Excellent Ladyship multiplied a hundredfold, and praying Our Lord to bless you and keep you happy always.   From San Matteo, the 14th of May 1633.

Your Most Affectionate Daughter,
SUOR M. CELESTE

From S. Casciano have come two deliveries totaling 8 *staia* [bushels] of flour for La Piera, but I did not try to pay for it, knowing there are other bills outstanding between you and Ninci.

Most Beloved Lord Father,
I have never let a courier pass this way without writing to you, Sire, and sending the letters to Signor Geri, who assures me that you must have received them by now. As for your returning here under these prevailing conditions, I can guarantee you neither resolution nor assurance on account of the contagious pestilence, whose end is so urgently desired that all the faith of the city of Florence is now vested in the Most Holy Madonna, and to this effect this morning with great solemnity her miraculous image was carried from Impruneta to Florence, where it is expected to stay for 3 days, and we cherish the hope that during its return journey we will enjoy the privilege of seeing her.

We will hear what happens in any case, and next Saturday I shall give you a full report. Meanwhile, learning how the delay of your departure favors your interests, we more easily tolerate the sorrow that tries us during your absence.

In this neighborhood there have been two peasants infected by the evil pestilence, but at present no others are known, and now that all the gentlemen who own villas in the area have retreated to these parts, we take it as a sign that they suspect no sickness here.

I will be most grateful, for the love of Suor Luisa, if you would be so kind as to assist our dear old Confessor with his cause; but you will have to see, Sire, if you can talk about it to Signor Giovanni Mancini, who was sent the documents some time ago, though there has never been a response from him or from any of the others to whom this affair was referred.

I asked to have a little sample of the wine sent to me from your two recently filled casks, and it seems to me to be very good. La Piera tells me to have them refilled more often, but for quite a long time now they have not needed it.

Giuseppe is waiting to deliver these letters, so that I cannot add anything else, except that I implore you not to confuse yourself with drink, as I hear you have been doing. I greet you on everyone's behalf, and from the Lord God I pray your true happiness.   From San Matteo, the 21st of May 1633.

Your Most Affectionate Daughter,
Suor M. Celeste

Most Illustrious and Beloved Lord Father,
From the enclosure written to me today by Signor Rondinelli you will be able to gain full comprehension, Sire, of the conditions in Florence and its environs concerning the plague; and seeing as they are fairly good just now, and you almost fully released from your affairs, I truly hope that you will not have to delay your return to us much longer, as we are awaiting you with such longing; therefore I pray you not to let the ineffable

kindness of those most Excellent Lords bind you to them so tightly that we must be deprived of you for the whole summer. Great indeed has been their generosity up until now, nor will it ever be possible to repay all the favors and kindnesses bestowed on you and shared by us.

I want you to pay our usual respects to your hosts, Sire, especially to Her Most Excellent Ladyship the Ambassadress. Moreover I will be most appreciative if upon your return you will bring me a little starch, as you did the last time; and I remind you of the two portraits that I asked you for, a while ago.

As for the garden, according to what I hear from La Piera, the beans have formed the most beautiful verdure, climbing as tall as she is, but the fruit has been small and not very good, and the same for the artichokes, which I understand were much better last year: nonetheless there were enough for the house, for us, and also some went to Vincenzio and to Signor Geri. The orange trees still do not have a great quantity of flowers, and I expect the cold and wind that have dominated these past few days have done them considerable damage; those that fall, La Piera gathers and makes into juice. The lemons are so ripe that they require you, Sire, to come and harvest them, and from time to time, whenever one of them drops, it proves to be truly beautiful and most delicious.

This is as much as the duties of the apothecary will permit me to tell you, since Suor Luisa and another of my companions are purging themselves, and I am consequently alone at work. I send you loving regards from all our usual friends, and also from Suor Barbara and Suor Prudenza, and I pray the Lord God to keep you.   From San Matteo, the 28th of May 1633.

> Your Most Affectionate Daughter,
> SUOR M. CELESTE

Most Beloved Lord Father,
In my last letter I gave you good news regarding the plague, Sire, and now (God be praised and the Most Holy Madonna,

from Whom this grace is acknowledged) I give you even better
news, having learned that yesterday no one died of it and only
two went to the *lazaretto* [the plague hospital], sick with illnesses other than the contagion, sent there because the hospi-
tals do not take in such cases, or very few. I am not certain
whether people are still feeling well in the direction of Rovez-
zano; but this is a small thing, and with good management and
the help of the warm weather, which now makes its presence
felt intensely, we hope in short for a complete liberation.

In these regions no one is suspected of infection; the families
that suffered the greatest losses at the beginning of the out-
break are those of the Grazzini who are the workers of the Lan-
fredini, and the Farcigli, who lived halfway up the hill: there
was a large family divided among two or three houses, and
though I do not yet know whose workers they were, well I
know they are all dead. These are the confirmed reports that I
have diligently gathered so as to be able to keep you informed,
and thus encourage you to return, should you be dispatched
from all your affairs there. For indeed this period of your absence has worn on much too long, nor would I want you by
any means, Sire, to tarry until autumn, as I fear may happen, if
you wait too long to take your leave; all the more so since I
hear that you now find yourself free to pursue many recre-
ations, which gladdens and delights me greatly, while on the
other hand I am sorry that your pains give you no respite, although it seems almost requisite for the pleasure you take in
drinking those excellent wines to be counterbalanced by some
pain, so that, if you refrain from imbibing large quantities,
you may avoid some greater injury that could be incurred by
drinking.

In my last letter I did not have time to tell you how, during
its return from Florence, the image of the Most Holy Madonna
of Impruneta came into our Church; a grace truly worthy of
note, because she was passing from the Plain, so that she had to
come here, going back along the whole length of that road you
know so well, Sire, and weighing in excess of 700 *libbre* [about
one-quarter ton] with the tabernacle and adornments; its size
rendering it unable to fit through our gate, it became necessary
to break the wall of the courtyard, and raise the doorway of the

Church, which we accomplished with great readiness for such an occasion.

Suor Arcangela Landucci di San Giorgio [another first cousin, sister of Suor Chiara and Vincenzio Landucci], after having sent several times to demand two *scudi* from me with great entreaty, now writes me a long lament for the death of her Suor Sibilla, and implores me to beg you, Sire, as I am, that you do her the kindness of having a mass said for that soul at the altar of San Gregorio, as she needs such assurance to feel at peace, promising not to neglect you with her prayers.

Now that I have remembered San Gregorio, I am reminded that you never said anything to me, Sire, of having received a prescription I sent you for the plague. That struck me as strange, because it seemed to me I had offered you something useful, and I sincerely doubt that it has failed to do you good. And here, coming to an end by giving you loving greetings on behalf of our usual friends, I pray Our Lord to grant you His holy grace.   From San Matteo, the 4th of June 1633.

Sire's Most Affectionate Daughter,
SUOR M. CELESTE

Most Beloved Lord Father,
In my last letter, Sire, I said the situation regarding the contagion seemed well under control, but now I cannot in all honesty give a similar report, since for the past several days, the weather having turned unusually cool for this time of year, the plague has regathered its strength, and every day one hears of more houses being shut up, although the death toll is not that large, not exceeding seven or eight per day, as far as we can tell, with an equal number of people falling ill. Consequently, things having reached this pass, I would judge that you may still be able to travel in the direction of Siena, as you had intended, provided that your affairs can be concluded this month, because from then on till autumn no one will be allowed to frequent the open country around Rome, according to Signor Rondinelli;

and I surely would not want to see you forced, Sire, to make such a long sojourn so far away. Therefore please do everything you can to expedite your dispatch, which I still hope can be obtained as soon as possible with the help of blessed God and his Lordship the Ambassador, who clearly feels he can never do enough to aid and protect you, Sire, with all the forces at his command. [Although the hearings concluded on May 10, Galileo is still awaiting the outcome of his trial, at which time he expects to be able to leave Rome.] And truly, dearest Lord Father, if on the one hand the Lord God has afflicted and mortified you, He has then on the other relieved and assisted you greatly. Only to have conserved your health against the hardships you suffered through the journey, and since that time despite the torments you have endured, was in itself a most singular grace. May it please the Lord God to realize that we are not ungrateful for so many blessings, and to keep you and protect you till the very last, for which I pray Him with all my heart, and to you, Sire, I send a thousand loving greetings together with our dear ones.   From San Matteo, the 11th of June 1633.

    Sire's Most Affectionate Daughter,
    Suor M. Celeste

Most Beloved Lord Father,
When I wrote to you, Sire, giving you an account of the contagion's spread in this region, it had already very nearly ceased, for many days had run their course, weeks even, without anyone's hearing word of any new cases; and, as I suggested to you then, I felt entirely reassured by the knowledge that all those gentlemen neighbors of ours were staying here in their villas, as they still continue to do; and moreover, in the city of Florence itself, one heard that the pestilence was abating so appreciably that people were expecting they must soon be liberated from the whole misery. Wherefore, with this security, I moved to exhort you and implore you to return, although in my last letter,

hearing that things were taking a turn for the worse, I held my tongue, so to speak. Because, although it is very true that I have a strong desire to see you again, what I want much more is the preservation of your health and safety; and I recognize the special grace of the Lord God in the opportunity you have had, Sire, to remain where you are much longer than you and I would have wished. For even though I believe it must grieve you to stay on there so irresolutely, it would perhaps give you far more grief for us to be reunited among these perils, which in spite of everything continue on and may even be multiplying; and in consequence an order has come to our Monastery, and to others as well, from the Commissioners of Health, stating that for a period of 40 days we must, two nuns at a time, pray continuously day and night beseeching His Divine Majesty for freedom from this scourge. We received alms of 25 *scudi* from the commissioners for our prayers, and today marks the fourth day since our vigil began.

I have let Suor Arcangela Landucci know that you will perform the service she desires, Sire, and she thanks you profusely.

To give you news of everything about the house, I will start from the dovecote, where since Lent the pigeons have been brooding; the first pair to be hatched were devoured one night by some animal, and the pigeon who had been setting them was found draped over a rafter half eaten, and completely eviscerated, on which account La Piera assumed the culprit to be some bird of prey; and the other frightened pigeons would not go back there, but, as La Piera kept on feeding them they have since recovered themselves, and now two more are brooding.

The orange trees bore few flowers, which La Piera pressed, and she tells me she has drawn a whole pitcherful of orange water. The capers, when the time comes, will be sufficient to suit you, Sire. The lettuce that was sown according to your instructions never came up, and in its place La Piera planted beans that she claims are quite beautiful, and coming lastly to the chickpeas, it seems the hare will win the largest share, he having already begun to make off with them. The broad beans are set out to dry, and their stalks fed for breakfast to the little mule, who has become so haughty that she refuses to carry anyone, and has several times thrown poor Geppo [nickname for Giuseppe, Galileo's servant boy] so as to make him turn somersaults, but gently, since he was not hurt. Sestilia's brother Ascanio once asked to ride her out, though when he approached the gate to Prato he decided to turn back, never having gained the upper hand over the obstinate creature to make her proceed, as she perhaps disdains to be ridden by others, finding herself without her true master.

But returning to the garden, I tell you that although the grapevines appear very well, I do not know whether they will continue so, considering the abuse they take in being cared for at the hands of La Piera, instead of by yours, Sire. Only a few artichokes have shown themselves, yet surely we will dry one or two.

In the cellar everything is going well, the wine staying in good condition. In the kitchen I have no trouble providing what little the servants need, except when Signor Rondinelli comes, because then he wants to take care of everything, as for example this week he graciously arranged for us to dine one morning in the convent parlor with him. These are all the reports that I seem to be able to think of to share with you.

L'Archilea wants you to bring her, since there is such an abundance of good music teachers where you are, something beautiful to play on the organ. Suor Luisa is most eager to know if you have yet visited Signor Giovanni Mancini, the merchant, to settle the business for our dear old friend, and by the same token Suor Isabella would like to know if the letter that she sent you for Signor Francesco Cavalcanti has been delivered, as she wanted to learn from that gentleman if a brother of hers in those parts is dead or alive.

I close in order to keep something in reserve to tell you the next time I write, but I recall that I must give you greetings from Suor Barbera, and tell you, therefore, that she no longer ventures out except to enter the church by the first doorway to put up or and take down the hangings. All our other friends send you their regards, and I from blessed God pray for your every true good.   From San Matteo, the 18th of June 1633.

Sire's Most Affectionate Daughter,
SUOR M. CELESTE

Most Beloved Lord Father,
Thanks be to God that at last I hear you begin to speak of setting out on your journey home, which I have greatly desired
for so long, not solely to see you again, but also for the final
settlement of your affair, which must set your mind at ease and
peace. Surely you have not been able to feel such calm for many
months. But all the hardships you suffered may ultimately con-
fer blessings if they come to as good a conclusion as you lead
me to hope. [Unbeknownst to Suor Maria Celeste, Galileo faced
his sentencing by the Inquisition on June 22, at which time his
Dialogue was banned and he was censured and humiliated.]

I am very pleased that you are going to Siena, Sire, partly because you will avoid contact with the contagion of the plague,
which we understand, however, is somewhat alleviated this
week, and also because, hearing how that archbishop [Mon-
signor Ascanio Piccolomini, archbishop of Siena] invited you
with such insistence and kindness, I feel certain that you will
enjoy much pleasure and contentment there. Well I pray you to
proceed at your own convenience, and to afford yourself every
possible comfort, since you have now had to travel in two extremes of temperature, and also to give me news of yourself
whenever you can, just as you have done the entire time you
have been absent, for which I must thank you, this being the
greatest happiness I could have received under the circumstances.

I wanted to send along a letter for Her Ladyship the Ambassadress (to whom, for love of you, Sire, I know myself much
obliged), but because I suspect that, when this one arrives, you
will already have left, I am resolved to wait until next week, or
better, until you advise me when I should do it.

Of the service you performed for our dear old friend, Sire,
we will speak in person, if it pleases God, Whom I pray to
watch over you and protect you on this journey; and I greet
you lovingly with our usual friends.   From San Matteo, the
25th of June 1633.

Your Most Affectionate Daughter,
SUOR M. CELESTE

Most Illustrious and Beloved Lord Father,
Just as suddenly and unexpectedly as word of your new torment reached me, Sire, so intensely did it pierce my soul with
pain to hear the judgment that has finally been passed, de-
nouncing your person as harshly as your book. I learned all this
by importuning Signor Geri, because, not having any letters
from you this week, I could not calm myself, as though I already knew all that had happened.

My dearest lord father, now is the time to avail yourself more
than ever of that prudence which the Lord God has granted
you, bearing these blows with that strength of spirit which your
religion, your profession, and your age require. And since you,
by virtue of your vast experience, can lay claim to full cogni-
zance of the fallacy and instability of everything in this miserable world, you must not make too much of these storms, but
rather take hope that they will soon subside and transform
themselves from troubles into as many satisfactions.

In saying all that I am speaking what my own desires dictate,
and also what seems a promise of leniency demonstrated toward
you, Sire, by His Holiness, who has destined for your prison a
place so delightful, whereby it appears we may anticipate another commutation of your sentence conforming even more
closely with all your and our wishes; may it please God to see
things turn out that way, if it be for the best. [Although Galileo's
sentence consigned him to the dungeons of the Holy Office, his
friend Francesco Cardinal Barberini, the pope's nephew, immediately intervened and changed the place of his imprisonment to
the Tuscan Embassy. Within days, again thanks to Cardinal Barberini, Galileo was remanded to the palace of the archbishop of
Siena.] Meanwhile I pray you not to leave me without the consolation of your letters, giving me reports of your condition,
physically and especially spiritually: though I conclude my writing here, I never cease to accompany you with my thoughts and
prayers, calling on His Divine Majesty to grant you true peace
and consolation.   From San Matteo, the 2nd of July 1633.
Sire's Most Affectionate Daughter,
Suor M. Celeste

Most Illustrious and Beloved Lord Father,
That the letter you wrote me from Siena (where you say you find yourself in good health) brought me the greatest pleasure, and the same to Suor Arcangela, is needless for me to weary myself in convincing you, Sire, since you will well know how to fathom what I could not begin to express; but I should love to describe to you the show of jubilation and merriment that these mothers and sisters made upon learning of your happy return, for it was truly extraordinary; since the Mother Abbess, with many others, hearing the news, ran to me with open arms, and crying with tenderness and happiness; truly I am bound as a slave to all of them, for having understood from this display how much love they feel for you, Sire, and for us. Hearing furthermore that you are staying in the home of a host as kind and courteous as Monsignor Archbishop multiplies the pleasure and satisfaction, despite the potential prejudicial effect this may have on our own interests, because it could well prove to be the case that his extremely enjoyable conversation may engage and detain you much longer than we would like. However, since here for now the suspicions of contagion continue, I commend your remaining there and awaiting (as you say you wish to do) the safety assurance from your closest friends, who, if not with greater love, at least with more certainty than we possess, will be able to apprise you of the facts.

But meanwhile I should judge that it would be wise to draw a profit from the wine in your cellar, at least one cask's worth; because although for now it is keeping well, I fear this heat may precipitate some peculiar effect: and already the cask that you had tapped before you left, Sire, from which the housemaid and the servant drink, has begun to spoil. You will need to give orders as to what you want done, because I have so little knowledge of this business; but I am coming to the conclusion that since you produced enough to last the entire year, and as you have been away for six of those months, you will still have plenty left, even if you should return in a few days.

Leaving this aside, however, and turning to that which concerns me more, I am longing to know in what manner your affair was terminated to the satisfaction of both you and your adversaries, as you intimated in the next to last letter you wrote me from Rome: tell me the details at your convenience, and only after you have rested, because I can be patient awhile longer awaiting enlightenment on this contradiction.

Signor Geri was here one morning, during the time we suspected you to be in the greatest danger, Sire, and he and Signor Aggiunti went to your house and did what had to be done, which you later told me was your idea, seeming to me at the time well conceived and essential, to avoid some worse disaster that might yet befall you, wherefore I knew not how to refuse him the keys and the freedom to do what he intended, seeing his tremendous zeal in serving your interests, Sire. [Geri Bocchineri and the young mathematician Niccolò Aggiunti came to Arcetri to remove possibly incriminating papers from Galileo's house.]

Last Saturday I wrote to her ladyship the Ambassadress with all the great love that I felt, and if I receive an answer, I shall share it with you. I close here because sleep assails me now at the third hour of the night [near 11 P.M.], on which account you will excuse me, Sire, in the event I have said anything inappropriate. I return to you doubled all the regards you offered to those named in your letter and especially La Piera and Geppo, who are thoroughly cheered by your return; and I pray blessed God to give you His holy grace.   From San Matteo, the 13th of July 1633.

Sire's Most Affectionate Daughter,
Suor M. Celeste

Most Illustrious and Beloved Lord Father,
I saw the letter from Signor Mario with greatest pleasure, having thus understood your condition, Sire, regarding your inner peace of mind, and with this my soul is also soothed and calmed to a large extent, but not entirely, given the vast distance between us and the uncertainty of when I will see you

again: and here we observe a certain truth, that one cannot find genuine tranquility and contentment in any worldly thing. When you were in Rome, Sire, I said to myself: if I have the grace of your leaving that place and coming as far as Siena I will be satisfied, for then I can almost say that you are in your own house. And now I am not content, but find myself longing to again have you here even closer. Be that as it may, blessed be the Lord for having granted us His grace so magnanimously until now. It falls to us to try to be truly grateful for this much, so that He may be the more favorably disposed and compassionately moved to bless us in other ways in the future, as I hope He will do by His mercy. Meanwhile I pray most fervently for one thing above all others, Sire, which is the preservation of your health in the face of all the torments you have survived.

Neither the time nor the occasion permits me to write at greater length just now. Upon receipt of another letter from you, which indeed must soon reach me, I will write longer and give you a detailed report about the house.

I send you regards on behalf of all our usual friends and Signor Rondinelli who treats us so tenderly; and from the Lord God I pray for your consolation.   From San Matteo in Arcetri, the 16th of July 1633.

   Sire's Most Affectionate Daughter,
   SUOR M. CELESTE

Most Illustrious and Beloved Lord Father,
Signor Geri has not thus far been able to send me the letter that you wrote him, Sire, as he was required to leave it with the Grand Duke: he promised me he will try to let me have it before long. Meanwhile I am quite pleased with this one that you wrote to me, from which I understand that you are in good health, and enjoying every comfort and satisfaction, and for that I thank God, from Whom (as I have told you many times) I acknowledge your well-being as a special grace.

Yesterday morning I had some small samples taken of the wine from your casks, one of which is extremely good, the other has a bad color, and also the flavor does not seem right to me, almost as though it has spoiled. This evening I will tell Signor Rondinelli, who, following his usual Saturday custom, will be sure to come to the villa; and he will know better how to recognize whether drinking it may be bad for one's health, for the taste alone would not be all that unpleasant, and I will give you his opinion, Sire, so you can dictate what you want done, in the event it is not good. That white wine in the *fiaschi* is strong and will make an exquisite vinegar, except for the one in the small flask, which, on account of being only just beginning to spoil, we are drinking before it turns any worse: the defect was no fault of La Piera's, because she examined the bottles often and made sure to keep them filled. Quite a large quantity of capers was harvested and preserved, Sire, namely all those that were in the garden, for La Piera tells me you are especially fond of them.

There has not been any flour in your house for several days, but because this terrible heat makes it impossible to bake much bread, seeing as it hardens quickly and turns moldy, and it is not worth the effort of heating the oven to bake only a little bit, I have the boy buy it here in our shop.

With the next letter I will give you a more specific account of the daily expenditures, because now I lack the energy, succumbing (as is typical for me in this season) to extreme weakness, so that you might say I barely have the strength to move my pen. I greet you lovingly on behalf of all these reverend mothers, to whom every hour feels like a thousand years, on account of their strong desire to see you again, and I pray the Lord to bless you.   From San Matteo, the 23rd of July 1633.

Your Most Affectionate Daughter,
SUOR M. CELESTE

Most Illustrious and Beloved Lord Father,
I read the letter you wrote to Signor Geri with particular pleasure and consolation, Sire, on account of the things contained in its first section. I will be so bold as to venture on into the third

section as well, although it pertains to the purchase of some little house I do not know about, which I have inferred that Signor Geri very much wants Vincenzio to buy, albeit with your help. I certainly would not want to be presumptuous, interfering in matters that do not concern me. Nonetheless, because I care a great deal about whatsoever is of even minimal interest to you, Sire, I would implore you and exhort you (assuming you are in a position to be able to do this) to give them, if not the full amount, then some appreciable part of it, not only for love of Vincenzio, but just as much to keep Signor Geri favorably disposed toward you, as he has, on past occasions, shown great fondness for you, Sire, and, from all I have seen, tried to help you in any way he could: therefore, if, without too much trouble on your part, you could give him some sign of gratitude, I should judge that a deed well done. I know that you yourself can perceive and arrange such matters infinitely better than I, and perhaps I do not even know what I am saying, but well I know how anything I say is dictated by pure love toward you.

The servant who was in Rome with you came here yesterday morning, urged to do so by Signor Giulio Nunci. It seemed strange to me not to see letters from you, Sire. Yet I was appeased by the excuse this same man made, explaining that you had not known whether he would pass this way. Now that you are without a servant, Sire, our Geppo, who cannot move freely about here, desires nothing more, if only he were granted permission, than to come to you, and I should very much like that, too. If your thoughts concur, Sire, I could see to sending him well escorted, and I believe Signor Geri can secure him a permit to travel.

I also want to know how much straw to buy for the little mule, because La Piera fears she will die of hunger, and the fodder is not good enough for her, as she is a most original animal.

Since I sent you the list of expenses paid out for your house, we have incurred these others that I give you account of now, besides the money that every month I have made sure was paid to Vincenzio Landucci, for which I keep all the receipts, except the last two payments; for at those times he was, as he continues to be now, locked up in his house with the two little children because the plague killed his wife; whereby truly one may say she is released from her toil and gone to her rest, the poor woman. He sent early to ask me for the 6 *scudi* for the love of God, saying they were dying of hunger, and as the month was almost at its end I sent him the money; he promised the receipt when he is beyond suspicion of contagion, and I will endeavor to hold him to that; if nothing else I will first see to these other disbursements, in the event you are not here to take care of them yourself, Sire, which I suspect on account of the excessive heat that is upon us.

The lemons that hung in the garden all dropped, the last few remaining ones were sold, and from the 2 *lire* they brought I had three masses said for you, Sire, on my own initiative.

I wrote to her ladyship the Ambassadress, as you told me to, and sent the letter to Signor Geri, but I do not have a reply, wherefore I suppose I might be wise to write again suggesting the possibility that either my letter or hers has gone astray. And here, sending you love with all my heart, I pray Our Lord to bless you.   From San Matteo, the 24th of July 1633.

Your Most Affectionate Daughter,
SUOR MARIA CELESTE

Most Beloved Lord Father,
I am astonished that a courier has left you without any letters from me, as I have not failed to write them and forward them to Signor Geri, and this past week I wrote you two, Sire, one Saturday and one Monday: but perhaps by this time they have both reached you, and you are scrupulously informed of every household detail, as you wish. The sole unfinished business involves the wine, which, tasted by Signor Rondinelli, was decanted on his advice into another cask in order to remove it from the sediment: it will sit under watch for a few days, and, if it does not improve, then something else must be done before it spoils altogether: this concerns only the cask I had already

warned you was beginning to suffer, as the other for the time being maintains its good condition.

I have not neglected to prepare the aloe for you, Sire, and thus far I have poured the rose essence over it seven times; but because it is not yet dry enough to begin working into pill form, I send you for now a sample of those pills we produce for our apothecary shop, which contain the pure aloe washed only once with rose juice; nonetheless I do not believe that taking a single dose will do you any harm, even though the recipe has been altered somewhat.

As for how sorrowfully poor Landucci grieves over the death of his wife, I have no way of knowing, nor do I have any word of him except for what Giuseppe told me the day he went with Signor Rondinelli to deliver the 6 *scudi,* which was the 18th of this month; and he said that he set the money on the front steps and that he had only a glimpse of Vincenzio there inside the house quite far from the doorway, and that he looked sorely afflicted with an expression more of the grave than of life, and with him were the two little children, a boy and a girl, who are all that he has left of his family.

I am happy to hear that you keep your good health, Sire, and I pray you to endeavor to continue this way, by governing yourself well particularly with regard to the drinking that is so hurtful to you, for I fear that the intense heat and your social obligations to your host afford you ample opportunity for indulging with great risk of getting sick, which would only further postpone your ever so eagerly awaited return to us.

Our Lady Giulia, teacher of Suor Luisa and sister of Signor Corso, has in recent days locked arms with death, and although she is an old woman of 85 years, she has won out against all expectations, having been so seriously ill that we were on the verge of administering the last rites: now she is so far out of danger that she has not a trace of fever, and she sends a thousand regards to you, Sire, and all our friends do the same. May the Lord grant you His holy grace.   From San Matteo, the 28th of July 1633.

Sire's Most Affectionate Daughter,
Suor M. Celeste

Most Beloved Lord Father,
I write these few lines in great haste so as not to disobey your precept that I never let a week go by without writing.

As for the wine that was decanted, it seems to be quite improved in color, and La Piera finds it not at all unpleasant so she continues drinking it: we have finally found willing takers for the 3 barrels' worth that we must give away; 2 the smith will take, a half to Ambra's employee, and half for Domenico who works nearby on the Bini family's farm: we are looking to give away one more, because in the end I would not want to discard any of it, and the rest, which will be another barrel or a little more, will be consumed by the servants, because it does please them so, and also Suor Arcangela will not have to be begged to help them along.

In the dovecote there are two pairs of pigeon chicks waiting for you to come in person, Sire, to pronounce their final sentence. The harvest of lemons will prove fully satisfactory if the crop continues on like this, but the Seville oranges and the Portuguese oranges put out few flowers, and from those few only a tiny number matured; indeed there is not a single survivor from the whole grove.

The bread that can be bought for 8 *quattrini* is large and white. The straw for the mule will be provided: as for fodder, there is no point in thinking of it, because of the scarcity of grass this year, besides which, La Piera says, Madame Mule does not care for it much, but you may recall, Sire, how last year she used it to make her bed softer. Recently she has had some soreness in her mouth, because her stomach is so sensitive, they say, that drinking something cold may have made her sick, which has been a trial for La Piera. Now she is better.

You did well to open the letter from her most gracious Ladyship the Ambassadress, to whom I should like to be able to send for a present some delicacy together with the crystal, whenever the roads reopen. Signor Geri has not yet come by. For now I can say no more to you, Sire, except that I was most pleased with all the news you gave me in your last letter, concerning the tributes and satisfactions you are receiving over

there. And I greet you lovingly, and I pray Our Lord to bless you.   From San Matteo, the 3rd of August 1633.
   Your Most Affectionate Daughter,
   SUOR M. CELESTE G.

Most Beloved Lord Father,
Signor Geri was here yesterday morning for a parley with me to settle the business of the little house; and, as far as I was able to understand, he has no other interest beyond Vincenzio's advantage and benefit, which would be considerably advanced by this purchase, enabling him to increase the value and size of his own house, which may well seem to be closing in on him, in the event Vincenzio enlarges his family; moreover he says no one can live in the room over the cistern because it is unhealthy: and as for the question I raised as to whether Signor Geri had any thought of living there with Vincenzio, he answered that, while he might like to do so, he could not, as he needs to find more convenient lodgings closer to the Palace, for his sake as well as for those who come looking for him all day long, because this one on the Costa is too unsuitable and out of the way. As he stood firm on this point, I conclude that Signor Geri had wanted you to pay the full cost of the little house, which should not exceed 300 *scudi,* by his estimation: I repeated to him that it seemed neither possible nor appropriate for you, Sire, to take on this entire expense, as you understandably were short of money, having been confronted with expenses far beyond the ordinary, so I suggested to him that one might propose and pray you to contribute half the cost, if this were convenient for you, and then too, since he also says he will do his utmost to give the couple every possible advantage, providing the other half of the money would enable Signor Geri to help establish Vincenzio, until such time as he is able to repay the loan; to which Signor Geri yielded very promptly and politely, telling me that, although during your absence he has advanced other sums to Vincenzio, nevertheless he would have deprived himself if need be in order to lend him also these 150

scudi, to prevent this excellent opportunity from slipping through his fingers. This is how it transpired that a proposal comes before you, Sire, in the form I present to you now: it is up to you to decide, since you know far better than I how much you can afford to pay; I will only add that it has seemed incumbent upon me to involve myself in this business, which has been quite mortifiying for me, primarily because I would not want in the slightest way to disturb the peace that you tell me you are enjoying; which I fear may follow in any case, as you do not seem enthusiastically inclined to make this purchase. On the other hand, to entirely reject Signor Geri, who was appealing to you on behalf of your own son, and who shows such affection for you and for all our family, does not seem to me a laudable act. Please, Sire, by giving me an answer as soon as possible, free me from my uneasy state; and also let me know what effect the pills may have had, and whether you would like me to send you some more of the same type, as I have not yet been able to work with the aloe I prepared for formulating the new ones.

Suor Giulia returns your good wishes, and is eagerly awaiting, not the flask of white wine which you promised her, Sire, but rather you yourself; and the same for Signor Rondinelli, with whom I never fail to share the letters you write me, Sire, when I deem it permissible to do so; and here I give you my love, and pray your happiness from the Lord God.   From San Matteo, the 6th of August 1633.

Sire's Most Affectionate Daughter,
SUOR M. CELESTE

Most Beloved Lord Father,
If my letters, as you told me in one of yours, often reach you coupled in pairs, then I can tell you, not to repeat your exact words, that in this last post your letters arrived like the Franciscan friars wearing their wooden clogs, not only yoked together, but with a resounding clatter, creating in me a much greater than usual commotion of pleasure and happiness, Sire,

especially when I learned that my supplication on behalf of
Vincenzio and Signor Geri, which I submitted to you, or rather
urged upon you, to speak more accurately, has been agreed to
and settled so promptly and with even more generosity than I
had requested: and consequently I conclude that my importuning in no way posed a disturbance to your peace, for indeed
that possibility had worried me greatly, and now I feel cheered
and relieved and I thank you.

As for your return, God knows how much I desire it;
nonetheless, Sire, when you consider taking your leave from
that city, where it has suited you for some time to remain in a
place quite nearby, yet outside your own house, I should deem
it better for both your health and your reputation, to stay on
for several more advantageous weeks where for now you inhabit a veritable paradise of delights, especially considering the
enchanting conversation of that most illustrious Monsignor
Archbishop; rather than to have to return right away to your
hovel, which has truly lamented your long absence; and particularly the wine casks, which, envying the praise you have lav-
ished on the vintages of those other regions, have taken their
revenge, for one of them has spoiled its contents, or indeed the
wine has contrived to spoil itself, as I have already warned you
might happen. And the other would have done the same, had it
not been prevented by the shrewdness and diligence of Signor
Rondinelli, who by recognizing the malady has prescribed the
remedy, advising and working to bring about the sale of the
wine, which has been accomplished, through Matteo the merchant, to an innkeeper. Just today two mule loads are being decanted and sent off, with Signor Rondinelli's assistance. These
sales, I believe, must bring in 8 *scudi*: any surplus left over after the two loads will be bottled for the family and the convent
as we will gladly take this little bit: it seemed imperative to
seize such an expedient before the wine sprang any other sur-
prise on us that would have necessitated throwing it away.
Signor Rondinelli attributes the whole misfortune to our not
having separated the liquid from the sediment in the casks before the onset of the hot weather; something I did not know
about, because I am inexperienced in this enterprise.

The grapes in the vineyard already looked frightfully scarce before two violent hailstorms struck and completed their ruination. A few grapes were gathered in the heat of July before the arrival here of the highwaymen, who, not finding anything else to steal, helped themselves to some apples. On the feast day of San Lorenzo [August 10] there came a terribly destructive storm that raged all around these parts with winds so fierce that they wreaked great havoc, and touched your house as well, Sire, carrying away quite a large piece of the roof on the side facing Signor Chellini's property, and also knocking over one of those terra-cotta flower pots that held an orange tree. The tree is transplanted in the ground for the time being, until we have word from you as to whether you want another pot purchased to hold it, and we reported the roof damage to the Bini family [the landlords], who promised to have it repaired. The other fruit trees have borne practically nothing; particularly the plums, of which we had not a single specimen; and as for those few pears that were there, they have been harvested by the wind. However the broad beans gave a very good yield, which, according to La Piera, will amount to 5 *staia* and all of them beautiful: now come the beans.

It would behoove me to give you an answer concerning your inquiry about whether or not I sit idle; but I am saving that until some time when I cannot sleep, as it is now the third hour of the night [near 11 P.M.]. I send you greetings on behalf of everyone I have mentioned, and even more from Doctor Ronconi who never comes here without pressing me for news of you, Sire. May the Lord God bless you.   From San Matteo, the 13th of August 1633.

 Sire's Most Affectionate Daughter,
 Suor M. Celeste

Most Beloved Lord Father,
When I wrote to you about your coming home soon, Sire, or your otherwise remaining where you are for a while longer, I

knew of the petition you had made to his lordship the Ambassador, but was not yet aware of his answer, which I since learned from Signor Geri when he came here last Tuesday, just after I had written yet another letter to you, enclosing the recipe for the pills that by now must surely have reached you. My motive for addressing you in that seemingly distant fashion had grown out of my frequent discussions with Signor Rondinelli, who all through this period has been my refuge (because, as practical and experienced as he is in the ways of the world, he has many times alleviated my anxiety, prognosticating for me the outcome of situations concerning your affairs, especially in cases that seemed more precipitous to me than they later turned out to be); once during those discussions he told me how people in Florence were saying that when you departed from Siena, Sire, you would have to go to the Certosa [a monastery south of Florence], a condition that displeased every one of your friends; yet he saw some good in going along with those orders, as I understand the Ambassador himself did, too, for they both suspected that soliciting too urgently for your direct return here, Sire, might bring about some negative consequence, and therefore they wanted to allow more time to elapse before entreating again. Whereupon I, fearing the worst could all too easily come to pass, and hearing you were preparing to petition yet again, set myself to write to you as I did. If ever I fail to make a great demonstration of the desire I harbor for your return, I refrain only to avoid goading you too much or disquieting you excessively. Rather than take that risk, all through these days I have been building castles in the air, thinking to myself, if, after these two months of delay in not obtaining the favor of your release, I had been able to appeal to her Ladyship the Ambassadress, then she, working through the sister-in-law of His Holiness, might have successfully implored the Pope on your behalf. I know, as I freely admit to you, that these are poorly drawn plans, yet still I would not rule out the possibility that the prayers of a pious daughter could outweigh even the protection of great personages. While I was wandering lost in these schemes, and I saw in your letter, Sire, how you imply that one of the things that fans my desire for your return is the anticipation of seeing myself delighted by a certain present you are bringing, oh! I can tell you that I turned truly angry; but enraged in the way that blessed King David exhorts us in his psalm where he says, *Irascimini a nolite peccare* [Be angry, but sin not]. Because it seems almost as though you are inclined to believe, Sire, that the sight of the gift might mean more to me than that of you yourself: which differs as greatly from my true feelings as the darkness from the light. It could be that I mistook the sense of your words, and with this likelihood I calm myself, because if you questioned my love I would not know what to say or do. Enough, Sire, but do realize that if you are allowed to come back here to your hovel, you could not possibly find it more derelict than it is, especially now that the time approaches to refill the casks, which, as punishment for the evil they committed in allowing the wine to spoil, have been hauled up onto the porch and there staved according to the sentence pronounced by the most expert wine drinkers in these parts, who point out as the primary problem your practice, Sire, of never having broken them open before, and these same experts claim the casks cannot suffer now for having had some sunshine upon their planks.

I received 8 *scudi* from the sale of the wine, of which I spent 3 on 6 *staia* of wheat, so that, as the weather turns cooler, La Piera may return to her bread baking; La Piera sends her best regards to you, and says that if she were able to weigh your desire to return against her longing to see you, she feels certain her side of the scale would plummet to the depths while yours would fly up to the sky: of Geppo there is no news worthy of mention. Signor Rondinelli this week has paid the 6 *scudi* to Vincenzio Landucci and has retained two receipts, one for last month, one for this: I hear that Vincenzio and the children are healthy, but as for their welfare I do not know how they are getting along, not having been able to inquire after them from a single person. I am sending you another batch of the same pills, and I greet you with all my heart together with our usual friends and Signor Rondinelli. May Our Lord bless you. From San Matteo in Arcetri, the 20th of August 1633.

Sire's Daughter,
SUOR MARIA CELESTE

Most Beloved Lord Father,
I live with the hope that the favor you are seeking to obtain, Sire (under those conditions you wrote about) will be granted to you; and it seems to me to be taking a thousand years to hear what answer will be handed down, so that I beseech you to notify me immediately of the outcome even if it runs contrary to our wishes; though I surely do not want to believe anything else could go wrong.

I have news for you of how, through the death of Signor Benedetto Parenti, which occurred last Wednesday, our Monastery has inherited a farm at Ambrogiana, and our procurator went that very same night to take possession of it. Several people have estimated its value at more than five thousand *scudi,* and they also say that this year's harvest will yield 16 *moggia* of wheat along with 50 barrels of wine and 70 sacks of millet and other grains, so that my convent will be greatly relieved.

The day before I received the letter from you, Sire, Master Ceseri [father-in-law of Galileo's sister Livia] borrowed the little mule to go to Fiesole, and Geppo told me how that evening he brought her back to the house completely unshod and badly handled, so that I have enjoined Geppo, in the event Master Ceseri may return to request her again, to refuse him politely, alleging the orneriness of the little beast along with your desire, Sire, that she not be flayed alive.

For the past several weeks La Piera has had no needlework to do in the house, and if it is true what I hear that very good quality linen can be had where you are, Sire, you might see about buying a small quantity of it; for if it is indeed fine, it will be the best thing for making handkerchiefs, pillowcases and similar items: and I want you to procure me a bit of saffron for the apothecary, since it is called for in the formulation of the papal pills, as you will have noticed.

I am not feeling entirely well, and this accounts for my writing so disjointedly. I commend you to God, may He be the One to give you every consolation.   From San Matteo, the 27th of August 1633.

Your Most Affectionate Daughter,
SUOR M. CELESTE

Most Beloved Lord Father,

Hearing the discussion of your going into the countryside brings me pleasure for your sake, Sire, knowing as I do how much the rural lifestyle both suits and delights you, though I am sorry for us, seeing that your return will be further delayed: but may it all turn out as you wish, for as long as the grace of blessed God keeps you healthy and happy, all the other problems are tolerable, rather they become gentle and enjoyable with the hope I cherish that on account of these mortifications sent to you and to us by the Lord God, in His supreme wisdom, you stand ready to draw great good from them through His mercy.

The disgrace of the wine was a blow for you, Sire, and I am prepared to call it an even worse one for us, because, wanting to preserve the contents of the casks, we never drank a drop of their contents, and even from the one you left newly tapped we took very little, since it quickly grew too fiery to suit us, and that little of the white, after waiting too long for you, Sire, became vinegar: there are six flasks in the house left over from the wine we sold, and this is good enough for the servants: the remainder from the first cask was discarded because that wine had gone completely sour, and I did not want them to drink it: until your new vintage is ready they will need to buy wine by the flask, and I will implore Signor Rondinelli to direct Geppo where to go to find the variety most appropriate for them.

The little mule has been provided with three loads of extremely good straw, for which we paid seven *lire* and four *crazie* each; fodder this year was simply unavailable, not to mention that it does not satisfy the dear creature.

A long time ago I sent the boy to retrieve the clock, but the maestro would not give it to him, saying that he wanted to wait until you came back, Sire; yesterday I sent word again to tell him to return it in any case, and he said that first he needed to look it over again, and so he will, and if perchance he should still not release it, I will order the boy to stop in with Signor Rondinelli.

Lord Father, I must inform you that I am a blockhead, indeed the biggest one in this part of Italy, because seeing how you wrote of sending me seven "buffalo eggs" I believed them truly to be eggs, and planned to make a huge omelette, convinced that such eggs would be very grand indeed, and in so doing I made a merry time for Suor Luisa, who laughed long and hard at my foolishness. ["Buffalo eggs" are the egg-shaped lumps of mozzarella cheese made from water buffalo milk.] Tomorrow morning, which will be Sunday, the boy will go to San Casciano to pick up the packages, as you ordered, Sire; meanwhile I offer my thanks for all the things that you say are in them.

When you return here, Sire, you will not find Signor Donato Gherardini, rector of Santa Margherita and brother of our Suor Lisabetta, because he died two days ago, and as yet we do not know who will succeed him.

Suor Polissena Vinta had wanted to know if, among the several well-known relief efforts being undertaken where you are, any help has been forthcoming from Signor Cavalier Emilio Piccolomini, the son of Captain Carlo who was married to the niece of our same Suor Polissena; who, in order to be able to commend this man to the Lord in her prayers, wants to discover several facts through your help, Sire, since many things that are said of him are simply incredible; nor can one believe them to be aught but lies and fables spawned by rumor.

I made sure that the two letters you enclosed were forwarded immediately to their rightful recipients; more I cannot tell you if not that, when I receive your letters, I no sooner read them than I begin looking for another courier to come bearing still more of them, and especially now that I await certain words from Rome.

The Mother Abbess, Signor Rondinelli, and all the others return your regards doubled, Sire, and from Blessed God I pray that you receive an abundance of Heavenly grace.   From San Matteo, the 3rd of September 1633.

Your Most Affectionate Daughter,
SUOR MAR. CELESTE

Most Illustrious Lord Father,
Last Thursday, and also Friday until nightfall, I stood with my soul in suspense, seeing that your letters were not going to arrive, not knowing to what cause I could arrogate that silence. When later I received them, and thus learned that Monsignor Archbishop was well aware of my gaffe regarding the buffalo eggs, I could not help but blush for shame, although on the other hand I am happy to have given you grounds for laughter and gladness, as it is with this motive I so often write to you of foolish things.

I have consoled Mother Vinta with the reassuring news you gave me of her great-nephew, Sire, and when she learned the details of that self-same magnanimous man's charitable acts, she became sorely resentful, saying that not only Signor Emilio but also his mother Elisabetta never give a thought or a penny to her, so that she believes they assume she must be dead: and yet you know how needy she is, Sire, being almost continuously sick in bed.

I received the bags with all the things that you wrote you were sending: the buffalo eggs I have shared with our friends here and also with Signor Rondinelli; the saffron was excellent and more than enough to make the pills, for which I have purified about 4 or 5 ounces of aloe, sure to be of the best quality for my having run it over the rose water seven times. The very next opportunity I have to write, which I will find before Tuesday, I will send you some of the preparation I want to make fresh today or tomorrow, provided that the headache and toothaches, which I endure at the moment, will ease enough, for now they force me to leave off writing, while I continue always to commend you to the Lord God as the One to grant you true consolation.   From San Matteo, the 10th of September 1633.

    Sire's Most Affectionate Daughter,
    SUOR MAR. CELESTE

Most Beloved Lord Father,

I was thinking of playing a wonderful prank on you, Sire, which was to have our Geppo arrive unexpectedly on that distant doorstep; but, from what I understand, Signor Geri has foiled my plan by warning you all about it. I have had this wish ever since you got to Siena. Recently I resolved at last to carry it out, and yesterday by my good fortune a proclamation went into effect including the freeing of roadways all around the region, for so I am advised by Signor Rondinelli, who also told me he did not give away this fact in his letter, Sire, because the ruling had not yet been made public when he wrote to you. I believe that you will be happy to see the boy, to have trustworthy news of us, with an equally detailed report of the house, and we on the other hand shall be especially pleased to hear of your welfare from someone who will actually have seen you. Meanwhile you can take some time to determine your needs, be they linens or other items, and let him know, since I now have the means to send them safely.

As for the wine casks, the main subject of your letter to which I must respond, I will speak of them with Luca our worker before this evening, and implore him to go see them and take care of whatever may need to be done, because he strikes me as quite well informed in these matters.

The saffron seems perfection itself to Suor Luisa and me, and quite a bargain at 2 *lire* per ounce, owing of course to your kindness; and we have never before had any of such good quality, even at 4 *giuli* and 50 *soldi*.

The linen at 20 *crazie* per pound is a good value, although I do not believe it pays to buy it at that price for making plain cloths for the house; I gave a bundle to La Piera, telling her to spin it very fine; we will see how it turns out: that other for 4 *giuli* is indeed splendid, and several nuns here say they have paid up to half a *scudo* per pound for this type; if you could send us a little bit more of it, Sire, we will make some beautiful wimples.

Signora Maria Tedaldi was here last week with her widowed daughter, and she told me that now more than ever she longed for your return, Sire, finding herself in need of your help in the matter of remarrying that young woman, having the aim and desire to betrothe her to a certain member of the Talenti family with whom she has no better contact than through you, Sire, and if via a letter you thought you might be able to give her some assistance, she would like that a great deal; all this did she press me that I must convey to you, Sire, and thus do I tell you.

I am sending you a large quantity of the golden pills so you can give some away, and the round ones for you to take yourself as you need them.

I will be very happy to know if these few cakes I send along conform to your liking, though they have not turned out to my entire satisfaction, perhaps because of my wish to have everything I make for you succeed to the highest possible standards of excellence, which rarely happens for me: the candied citron morsels (which are at the bottom of the box) will perhaps by now be too hard for you, as I made them immediately after you arrived in Siena, hoping to be able to send them much sooner than this: do please save the box because it is not mine.

The list of expenses I enclose this time is much higher than the others; but it was not possible to curtail our spending. At least you will see, Sire, that Geppo does us honor with his good complexion, and has made a great effort to recover from that sickness he had. The 7 *lire* that I have earmarked as alms I gave for love of the Most Holy Madonna the morning of her birth [September 8] to someone who was in dire need, on the condition that she say certain prayers for you, Sire.

If you go off to the villa, as I hope, in the company of Monsignore, you will more easily be able to tolerate the remoteness of your own dear little hovel, so please do try to be cheerful, and if it seems to you that the time evaporates, as you wrote in one of your letters not long ago, so too, and very soon, it will take with it these days or weeks in which you must continue to stay on where you are, and then our mutual delight will be all the greater when we see each other again.

I urge you to guarantee the safe delivery of these accompanying letters, for they come from nuns who are our friends, who, together with the Mother Abbess, Suor Arcangela, and

Suor Luisa, send you their loving regards; and I pray Our Lord
to grant you the fulfillment of your every just desire.   From
San Matteo, the 17th of September 1633.

Sire's Most Affectionate Daughter,
SUOR MARIA CELESTE

I had forgotten to tell you that Suor Diamante would like to
know if you can find her some material for handkerchiefs of
the sort that I enclose herewith: if so, she would like you to do
her the service of buying a piece, and advising her of the cost so
she can repay you right away: the usual price near here would
be one *giulio,* 10 *crazie,* or more, depending on the fineness;
but now in Florence there is none to be had.

Most Beloved Lord Father,
I simply had to give you news of Giuseppe's return, Sire, as immediately as possible upon his arrival, which occurred yesterday after eight days' absence at the first hour of the night, for it
did not seem credible that in this many days I had not been able
to steal sufficient time to write you even four lines. Yet still that
is the truth, because, beyond the duties of my office, which at
present are numerous, Suor Luisa has suffered so fiercely with
her familiar stomach pain, that neither she nor those attending
her found a moment's rest day or night. And I especially felt
compelled by duty to wait on her without a single intermission.
Now that her improvement allows me to breathe somewhat, I
will also pay my debt to you, Sire, telling you that Geppo and
his father came home hale and hearty together with the little
mule, who really was dealt a great injustice being led off on
such a long journey; and I needed my anxiety allayed by the re-
assurances of those who know her better than I do. But enough
of that, she is fine.

I took the greatest delight in hearing the news the boy
brought me of your well-being, Sire, as he told me you looked
better than when you left here; which I can easily believe, be-

cause I judge that the comfort, the courtesy and charms that you have enjoyed, first in the house of his lordship the Ambassador in Rome, and now at the home of that most illustrious Monsignor Archbishop, have been pleasantly powerful enough to mitigate almost all the bitterness of those distasteful events now past, and for this reason you have not felt any harm. And now in particular, how could you not bless this prison you inhabit, and deem your detention a most felicitous one? especially if it affords you the opportunity to enjoy even more frequently and with ever greater intimacy the conversation of such a renowned prelate and such a benevolent gentleman? And they, not content to exercise all the kind regards that one could most desire upon your person, Sire, take it upon themselves to also favor us poor nuns with affectionate words and the most loving demonstrations, for which I do not doubt you have rendered them due thanks on our behalf: wherefore I will not repeat them, except that I would like you, Sire, offering them the most humble reverence in our names, to assure them that with our prayers we will ever endeavor to render ourselves grateful for all these favors.

As for your homecoming, if all conforms to your hope and our desire, it will surely happen soon. Meanwhile I tell you that the casks for the red wine are all ready, even including the one that held the spoiled wine, though it had to be taken apart and cleaned with particular care: for the white wine Signor Rondinelli has seen that 3 casks are in extremely good condition, while there is one among the others that last year held the Greek wine, from which they drew I think 4 or 5 flasks' worth with a very strong taste, as I understand; and since some wine still remains at the bottom, the cask has not had a chance to dry; Signor Rondinelli says it will be well to give them all a good cleaning before putting any wine inside, but they are otherwise excellent.

The Mother Abbess thanks you profusely for the saffron and I for the other gifts, namely the linen, the hare, and the Spanish bread, which is truly delicious.

I will have Geppo deliver the rosary and the slippers for your cousin.

Doctor Giovanni Ronconi, who comes by very often to visit five nuns who have been sick for some time now, all suffering from the fever, told me the other day that he did not believe I had ever given you his regards, Sire, and I answered him that indeed I had done so, and at least in my imagination this took place more than once. It is very true that I was delinquent in never conveying your regards, Sire, to him, wherefore I pray you to do me the favor of making good my error, by writing him two lines and sending them to me, so that I will be able to forward them to him, since I have occasion every day to give him a report of these feverish patients, and truly he has never once been here that he has not asked after you and shown great compassion for your troubles.

I would have liked to have been able to gauge your need, Sire, in terms of money, so as to be able to send you the right amount; I believe however that by now you have already received a sum sent by Signor Alessandro [Bocchineri, brother of Geri and Sestilia], as I understood from a letter you wrote to him, and which he sent me to stand in for the one that was to have reached me this week, and that perhaps you did not send me as revenge for my not writing you; but now you have heard the reason: and here I bid you farewell and wish you a good night, of which precisely half has already passed.   From San Matteo in Arcetri, the first of October 1633.

Your Most Affectionate Daughter,
SUOR M. CELESTE

Most Beloved Lord Father,
Saturday I wrote to you, Sire, and Sunday, thanks to Signor [Niccolò] Gherardini [a young follower, and later biographer, of Galileo, and relative of Suor Elisabetta], your letter was delivered to me, through which, learning of the hope you hold out for your return, I am consoled, as every hour seems a thousand years to me while I await that promised day when I shall see you again; and hearing that you continue to enjoy your

well-being only doubles my desire to experience the manifold happiness and satisfaction that will come from watching you return to your own home and moreover in good health.

I would surely not want you to doubt my devotion, for at no time do I ever leave off commending you with all my soul to blessed God, because you fill my heart, Sire, and nothing matters more to me than your spiritual and physical well-being. And to give you some tangible proof of this concern, I tell you that I succeeded in obtaining permission to view your sentence, the reading of which, though on the one hand it grieved me wretchedly, on the other hand it thrilled me to have seen it and found in it a means of being able to do you good, Sire, in some very small way; that is by taking upon myself the obligation you have to recite one time each week the seven psalms, and I have already begun to fulfill this requirement and to do so with great zest, first because I believe that prayer accompanied by the claim of obedience to Holy Church is effective, and then, too, to relieve you of this care. Therefore had I been able to substitute myself in the rest of your punishment, most willingly would I elect a prison even straiter than this one in which I dwell, if by so doing I could set you at liberty. Now we have come this far, and the many favors we have already received give us hope of having still others bestowed on us, provided that our faith is accompanied by good works, for, as you know better than I, Sire, *fides sine operibus mortua est*. [faith without works is lifeless.]

My dear Suor Luisa continues to fare badly, and because of the pains and spasm that afflict her right side, from the shoulder to the hip, she can hardly bear to stay in bed, but sits up on a chair day and night: the doctor told me the last time he came to visit her that he suspected she had an ulcer in her kidney, and that if this were her problem it would be incurable; the worst thing of all for me is to see her suffer without being able to help her at all, because my remedies bring her no relief.

Yesterday they put the funnels in the six barrels of rose wine, and all that remains now is to refill the cask. Signor Rondinelli was there, just as he also attended the harvesting of the grapes, and told me that the must was fermenting vigorously so that he hoped it would turn out well, though there is not a lot of it; I do not yet know exactly how much. This is all that for now in great haste I am able to tell you. I send you loving regards on behalf of our usual friends, and pray the Lord to bless you. From San Matteo in Arcetri, the 3rd of October 1633.

Sire's Most Affectionate Daughter,
SUOR M. CELESTE

Most Beloved Lord Father,
Signor Rondinelli, who inspected the kegs of white wine again, told me there were three extremely good ones, as I notified you, Sire, and then, when I questioned him about their capacity, he replied that I had no need to inform you about this, because you already knew roughly what that was: he assured me there were additional kegs, but that he did not feel he could promise them to be of the same quality: this week he has not been able to come up here, nor has it been possible for him, on that account, to make another new assessment; but I have made one myself which I do not think will displease you, and it is this, that in our cellar are 3 or 4 casks of various sizes, one of 6, one of 5 and the other of 4 barrels in capacity, which every year we fill with our white verdea wine, as is our custom, but because this year we did not make even one drop of it, I have reserved them for you, Sire, because I am certain they are sound, with the authority to deliver them to your wine cellar so they can be filled there when you send the wine, and for the wine to be left in those casks until you can decant it yourself in your own way, or for the entire year, if that seems best: you can in any event let me hear your thoughts on all this. The wine from San Miniato has not yet been distributed: in return for the wine we gave away, meanwhile, we have recovered one barrel from the farmers here, and had it put into the cask which formerly held that spoiled wine; which cask was of course first set to rights; the wine from your vines has not yet been drawn from the fermenting vat: at my behest, Signor Rondinelli had a word with

the blacksmith about the 3 barrels that he owes us, and brought back his solemn promise on that score.

It was not that I kept silent about the receipt of the 6 wheels of cheese, Sire, but rather that my language, for being very coarse, must have escaped your comprehension, since I had every intention of including you, or to say it better, acknowledging you, in the thanks that I said I wanted you to extend on our behalf to Monsignor Archbishop, from whom you wrote that the gift had come. I meant to do the same in regard to the buffalo eggs, but, assuming they were intended for Geppo and his father, I left the whole lot to them, and said no more about it. I should also have thanked you for the most excellent wine that Monsignore sent us, which almost every one of the nuns has tasted, and Suor Giulia made her portion into a soup.

I thank you, too, for the letter you sent me for Doctor Ronconi, which, after having read it myself with great pleasure, I sealed and delivered into his hands yesterday morning, where it was received most courteously.

I am delighted to hear of your good health and peace of mind, and that your pursuits are so well suited to your tastes, as your current writing seems to be, but for love of God may these new subjects not chance to meet the same luck as past ones, already written.

I want to know if you are still enjoying the conversation of Monsignor Archbishop, or if he has gone off to the villa, as Geppo told me he had heard would happen; an event that I feel certain would have caused you considerable mortification.

Suor Luisa remains in bed surrounded by physicians and physics, but the pains are somewhat mitigated with the help of the Lord God, whom I pray, Sire, to grant you His holy grace. I give you greetings from everyone here, and I commend you to God.   From San Matteo in Arcetri, the 8th of October 1633.

Your Most Affectionate Daughter,
S. Mar. Celeste

La Piera has just this moment told me that the wine from your vines will amount to one barrel and 2 or 3 flasks, and that she plans to mix it with that from the local farmers, because by itself it is very weak: the San Miniato wine is expected today, or so the servant of Signor Niccolò [Aggiunti] said up till the day before yesterday, and now I believe him.

Most Beloved Lord Father,
The wine from San Miniato has still not arrived, and so I wrote three days ago to Signor Geri, who responded that he would try to learn from Signor Aggiunti the cause of this delay. I have not heard anything more as yet, because this week I have missed the opportunity to send Geppo to Florence, as he was, and still is, at San Casciano with Master Giulio Ninci, who fell ill many days ago, and because there was no one to care for him, Master Alessandro [Ninci] sought me out to ask if I would grant them our boy's help for a while, which request I knew not how to deny.

I have tasted the Rose wine. When the Canon sends someone to collect the money for the wine, I will carry out your orders, Sire.

Signor Gherardini was here recently to visit his relative, Suor Elisabetta, and had me called as well to give me news of you, Sire. He shows himself to be enormously fond of you; and he told me that ever since he spoke to you peace has entered his heart, which formerly had been ruled by uncertainty and anxiety over your trials. May it please Blessed God that the final decree regarding your return does not postpone it longer than we hope, so that you may enjoy, in addition the comfort of your own home, the conversation of this impressively accomplished young man.

But meanwhile I take endless pleasure in hearing how ardently Monsignor Archbishop perseveres in loving you and favoring you. Nor do I suspect in the slightest that you are crossed out, as you say, *de libro viventium* [from the book of the living], certainly not throughout most of the world, and not even in your own country: on the contrary it seems to me from what I hear that while you may have been eclipsed or erased very briefly, now you are restored and renewed, which is a thing that stupefies me, because I am well aware that ordinarily: *Nemo proféta accettus est in patria sua* [No one is accepted as prophet in his own country]. (I fear that my wanting to use the Latin phrase has perhaps made me utter some barbarism.) And surely, Sire, here at the convent you are also beloved and esteemed more than ever; for all this may the Lord God be praised, as He is the principal source of these graces, which I consider my own reward, and thus I have no other desire but to show gratitude for them, so that His Divine Majesty may continue to concede other graces to you, Sire, and to us as well, but above all your health and eternal blessing.

Suor Luisa is confined to bed with a slight fever, yet the pains have abated appreciably, and we hope that she will be freed of them completely with the help of good medicaments, which, if they are not as sweet to the taste as the wine you are drinking, under these circumstances they are more useful and necessary.

The moment I saw the 6 wheels of cheese, I allocated half of them to you, Sire, but I did not write as much to you because I wanted this to be a matter of action more than words: and truly the taste is something scrumptious, and I am eating a little more than I should.

I sent the letter to Tordo via our steward, who learned from the man's wife that he is in the hospital taking the wood cure, thus it is no wonder you have not heard a response from him.

I have always wanted to know how to make those Sienese cakes that everyone raves about; now that All Saints' Day is approaching, you will have the occasion, Sire, to let me see them, I do not say "taste" them so as not to sound gluttonous: you are further obliged (because of the promise you made me) to send me some of that strong reddish linen yarn which I would like to use to start preparing some little Christmas gift for Galileino, whom I adore because Signor Geri tells me that, beyond being the namesake, the boy also has the spirit of his grandfather.

Suor Polissena received an answer to the letter you helped direct to her niece, Sire, and she also got a *scudo,* for which she thanks you in the enclosed: she prays for your eternal blessing, and sends you her regards, as do Madonna and our usual friends.

Signor Rondinelli has not shown his face here for a fortnight, because, from what I hear, he is drowning in a little wine which he had put in two kegs that are turning bad and giving him great grief.

I told La Piera to do some digging in the garden, so that she would be able to sow, or, to be more precise, set the broad beans.

A worker just arrived from Signor Niccolò Cini, who writes me four lines right on the same letter you wrote to him, Sire, informing me of the value of this wine, which was 19 *lire* per mule load and 2 *lire* for the carrying, 59 *lire* in all, and I remitted that amount. I have also written a short note to His Honor to thank him.

Nothing else weighs on me at the moment to tell you; rather I recall something I want to ask you, which is that I really must know whether Doctor Ronconi ever wrote back to you, for if he has not, I want to scold him about that the very next time I see him. May the Lord God be with you always.   From San Matteo in Arcetri, the 15th of October 1633.

Sire's Most Affectionate Daughter,
Suor M. Celeste

Most Beloved Lord Father,
Last Wednesday a brother of the Priory of San Firenze came to bring me a letter from you along with the little package of russet linen yarn, which, considering the rather thick quality of the thread, seems somewhat expensive; but indeed the color of the dye, being very beautiful, makes the price of 6 *crazie* per skein appear more tolerable.

Suor Luisa stays in bed with only the slightest improvement, and in addition to her, several of the others are also sick, so that if we now faced any suspicion of plague we would be lost. Among the sick is Suor Caterina Angela Anselmi who was formerly our Mother Abbess, a truly venerable and prudent nun, and, after Suor Luisa, the dearest and most intimate friend I have ever had: she is so gravely ill that yesterday morning she received the Extreme Unction, and it appears that she has only a few days to live; and the same must be said for Suor Maria Silvia Boscoli, a young woman of 22 years, and you may recall, Sire, how people once spoke of her as the most beautiful girl to grace the city of Florence for 300 years: this marks the sixth month she has been lying in bed with a continuous fever that the doctors now say has turned to consumption, and she is so wasted as to be unrecognizable; yet with all that she retains a vivacity and energy especially in her speech that astounds us, while from hour to hour we doubt whether that faint spirit (which seems entirely confined to her tongue) will fade away and abandon the already exhausted body: then, too, she is so listless that we can find no nourishment to suit her taste, or to say it better, that her stomach can accept, except a little soup made from broth in which we have boiled some dried wild asparagus, and these are extremely difficult to find at this time of year, wherefore I was thinking that perhaps she could take some soup made from gray partridge, which has no gamy taste. And since these birds abound where you are, Sire, as you say in your letters, you might be able to send me one of them for her and for Suor Luisa, and I doubt you would encounter any difficulty having them reach me in good condition, since our Suor Maria Maddalena Squadrini recently received several fresh, good thrushes that were sent by a brother of hers who is Prior at the Monastery of the Angels, in part of the diocese very close to Siena. If, without too much trouble, Sire, you could help me make such a gift, now that the idea has whetted my appetite, I would be ever so grateful.

This time it devolves upon me to play the raven who bears bad tidings, as I must tell you that on the feast day of San Francesco [October 4], Goro, who worked for the Sertinis, died, and left a family in great distress, according to his wife who was here yesterday morning to beseech me that I must convey this news to you, Sire, and furthermore remind you of the promise you made to Goro himself and to Antonia his daughter, to give her a black woolen housedress when she got married: now they are in dire straits, and Sunday, which will be tomorrow, she will say her vows in Church; and because Goro's wife has spent what little money she had, first on medicaments and then for his funeral, she is hard-pressed, and wants to know if you can do her this kindness: I promised that I would tell her your answer as soon as I heard from you, Sire.

I would not know how to make you realize the happiness I derive from learning that you continue conserving your health in spite of everything, except to say that I enjoy your good fortune more than my own, not only because I love you more than myself, but also because I can imagine that if I were oppressed by infirmity, or otherwise removed from the world it would matter little or nothing to anyone, since I am good for little or nothing, whereas in your case, Sire, the opposite holds true for a host of reasons, but especially (beyond the fact that you do so much good and are able to help so many others) because the great intellect and knowledge that the Lord God has given you enables you to serve Him and honor Him far more than I ever could, so that with this consideration I come round to cheer myself and take greater pleasure from your well-being than from mine.

Signor Rondinelli has allowed himself to be seen again now that his kegs have quieted down; he sends his greetings to you, Sire, and so does Doctor Ronconi.

I assure you that I am never vexed by boredom, Sire, but sooner by the hunger caused, I believe, if not by all the exercise I perform, then by the coldness of my stomach, which does not get the full complement of sleep it requires, since I have no time. I rely on the oxymel and the papal pills to make up this deficit. I only tell you this to excuse myself for the haphazard appearance of my letter, as I was compelled to put down and then take up my pen again more than once before I could complete it, and on that note I commend you to God.   From San Matteo in Arcetri, the 22nd of October 1633.

Your Most Affectionate Daughter,
Suor M. Celeste

The enclosed conforms to the wish you expressed in your previous letter, Sire, that after having written to you I should write also to Her Ladyship the Ambassadress. I suspect that my numerous activities have sapped my energy, leaving me little to give her; you will be able to look it over and make corrections, and do let me know if you send her the ivory crucifix.

I still cling to the hope that this week you will have some resolution regarding your release, and I am burning with desire to share in that news.

Most Beloved Lord Father,
I delayed writing this week because I really wanted to send you the ortolans [small birds considered a delicacy], but in the end none has been found, and I hear they fly away when the thrushes arrive. If only I had known this desire of yours, Sire, several weeks ago, when I was racking my brain trying to think of what I could possibly send you that might please you; but never mind! You have been unlucky in the ortolans, just as I was foiled by the gray partridges, because I lost them to the goshawk.

Geppo returned yesterday from San Casciano, and brought the two boxes that you sent me, both in good condition; and since you have made me absolute proprietress over them, I take full advantage of this title, not sending more than half the items to my sister-in-law, although I did give another two cakes and two apricots to Signor Geri, telling him that you intended these, too, to be shared with La Sestilia: of the remainder I simply had to offer a portion to Signor Rondinelli, who shows himself so caring and cordial toward the two of us, as well as to many of our friends: these are all truly generous gifts, but also very costly ones, so that I would not be quite so willing another time to make a similar demand, which your munificence, Sire, has met more than four times over, and for which I multiply my thanks a hundredfold.

I made Goro's wife aware of your wish, Sire, to settle with her and provide charity upon your return; if later she comes to ask again, I will carry out your orders, and I will do the same with Tordo.

Young Ninci has recovered his health reasonably well and expressed his great satisfaction with the assistance he received from our Geppo. Suor Luisa is beginning to rise fairly often from her bed; Suor Caterina Angela died; the young consumptive nun holds on, but in a bad state.

The wine from San Miniato has not come, probably detained by the heavy rains, the same reason the broad beans have not been set in the garden, but they will be put in on the first day the weather turns fair; the lettuce and cabbage seeds have been sown, and there are also some onions; the artichokes are beautiful; of lemons we have an ample supply, though only a few oranges.

The little mule had some small discharge from one eye, but she is well now, as is La Piera her governess, who tends to the spinning and her praying to God that you come home soon, Sire: true as that is I cannot believe she puts her heart into her praying as much as I do. Although, while I hear that you feel so well, Sire, I know not what to tell myself, if not that the Lord reciprocates according to the great faith you place in my poor prayers, or, to speak more precisely, in one single prayer that I utter continuously with my heart, because I do not have time to speak it aloud with my voice. I send you no pills because desire makes me hope that you must soon arrive here to claim them in person: I am all eagerness to hear the resolution that will reach you this week. The comedy, coming from you, can be nothing if not wonderful; but as yet we have not been able to read past the first act. I do not lack for matters to discuss with you, but I do lack the time; and for this reason I close here, praying Our Lord and the Most Holy Madonna to be always in your company, and I greet you lovingly in the name of our usual friends. From San Matteo, the last of October of 1633.

Your Most Affectionate Daughter,
SUOR M. CELESTE

Most Illustrious Lord Father,
If only you were able to fathom my soul and its longing the
way you penetrate the Heavens, Sire, I feel certain you would
not complain of me, as you did in your last letter; because you
would see and assure yourself how much I should want, if only
it were possible, to receive your letters every day and also to
send you one every day, esteeming this the greatest satisfaction
that I could give to and take from you, until it pleases God that
we may once again delight in each other's presence. I believe
nonetheless that from those few lines I wrote you so hurriedly,
Sire, you could gather that they were written in the most lim-
ited time available, as I had none at all last Saturday when I
could render you your proper due; and I do have every good intention (if you will grant me this) of following through with
that tribute, because in these lamentations of yours I descry an
excess of affection that motivates them, and I glory in it. I did
try nevertheless to make good during the vigil of All Saints'
Day by sending you a letter via Signor Geri, and because I believe that one has already reached you, I will not reply exten-
sively to the questions you pose in this last one, except to say I
have received the packet for Master Ippolito [Tordo the lens-
maker], which you had not sent me previously: and as for
Geppo, to tell you that, after he brought me the boxes, he did
not return to San Casciano, because Il Ninci no longer needed
him: he will go back there in any case to see him again one day
this coming week.

Good fortune has attended my ardent wish, enabling me to
find the ortolans that you wanted, Sire, and I am just about to
consign the box, with flour inside it, to the boy, commissioning
him to go and get them at the game preserve, which is in the
Boboli Gardens [behind the Medici palace in Florence], from a
birdkeeper of the Grand Duke named Berna or Bernino, from
whom I bought them as a favor at one *lira* the pair, but judging
by what Geppo tells me after having seen them yesterday, they
are quite beautiful and to buy them from the poulterer would
cost as much as two *giuli*: Signor Rondinelli will then graciously do us the favor of packing them in the box, because the

boy would not have time to carry them all the way up here and then back down again once more, but will deliver them straight away to Signor Geri. May you enjoy them happily, Sire, and then tell me whether they were to your liking: there will be 20 as you wished.

I am called to the infirmary, wherefore I cannot say another word except that I send you my love together with the usual regards from the others, and especially Suor Luisa who fares considerably better, God be praised, and may He grant you, Sire, every true consolation.   From San Matteo, the 5th of November 1633.

    Your Most Affectionate Daughter,
    SUOR M. CELESTE

Most Beloved Lord Father,
Guccio the innkeeper, our neighbor here, comes to your vicinity to tend to business matters, and I seize the occasion to write you these few lines, Sire, telling you that if in my last letter I lauded the luck that made me find the ortolans, which I seemed at that moment to have in my grasp; now I lament that same luck for it did not land me the number I had wanted, as by now you will have seen for yourself, Sire, and also heard from Signor Geri: the reason was because among those that Il Berna had none were of good quality except for that group of eleven that we sent; and since Geppo had made the blunder of accepting these few, after I had searched for other sources around the countryside and in Florence, I resolved to send them to you, encouraged by the gamekeeper at the villa of the Poggio Imperiale [the Medici palace in Arcetri], who said to consider them as grand gifts at this time of year now that they are so rare; enough: if nothing else, Sire, you will accept my good will.

Master Ippolito asked for the 4 *scudi,* and I sent them to him right away.

The wine from San Miniato has still not arrived. The garden cannot be worked, because it is too wet. The boy went today to look in on Il Ninci again.

Suor Luisa is better, but not entirely well; she greets you lovingly, Sire, and so do Suor Arcangela, Madonna, Suor Cammilla and her papa, who has not let himself be seen around here for quite some time on account of the bad weather, but writes often. May Our Lord preserve you.   From San Matteo, the 7th of November 1633.

Your Most Affectionate Daughter,
SUOR M. CELESTE

Most Beloved Lord Father,
Taking advantage of the opportunity to write to you again, Sire, via this worker for Sir Santi Bindi who is setting out in your direction, I must tell you first how astounded I was that you made no mention in your most recent letter of having received any word from Rome, nor any resolution regarding your return, which we had so hoped to have before All Saints' Day, from what Signor Gherardini led me to believe. I want you to tell me truly how this business is progressing, so as to quiet my mind, and also please tell me what subject you are writing about at present: provided it is something that I could understand, and you have no fear that I might gossip.

Tordo has received the 4 *scudi,* as I wrote to you last Thursday, and the Bini family sent their worker Domenico to collect the rent for the house: I replied that their request will be satisfied the moment you are made aware of it, Sire, and you give me your orders.

No one has been able to work in the garden more than half a day in all this time, because the weather has been so hostile, which I think explains why you feel thus afflicted, Sire, by your pains.

The two pounds of linen that you sent with Geppo seemed the same quality as the previous batch at 20 *crazie,* which turned out very well, but considering the cost I believe this lot could be better; the single pound at 4 *giuli* is extremely fine and not overpriced.

Master Giulio Ninci feels altogether well, from what Geppo

tells me, and has sent us some very thoughtful gifts: and Master Alessandro his cousin gave me a citron, from which I have made these 10 sweets I am sending you, each of which, for being slightly aromatic will prove pleasing, if not to the taste, then to the stomach. You will be able to sample them, Sire, and, if you deem it fitting, present them to our Most Illustrious Monsignor together with the rose. The pine nut cake with the two pieces of quince pear I received from my Suor Ortensia, and in exchange I gave her one of those Sienese cakes I requested of you, Sire.

I send you no pills because I have not had time to reformulate them, aside from the fact that I sense you have no need of them.

When the bearer of this letter returns I will be expected to reward him kindly for having carried out my request; I would value your advice, Sire, as to what I might give him to compensate him yet not overpay him: since he travels to that region principally to serve his own needs.

I end by giving you the usual greetings, and from the Lord God I pray for your true contentment.   From San Matteo, the 12th of November 1633.

Your Most Affectionate Daughter,
Suor M. Celeste

The continuous rain has not allowed Giovanni (as the bearer of this letter is called) to leave this morning, which is Sunday, and this leaves me time to chat with you a little longer, and to tell you that recently I pulled a very large molar, which had rotted and was giving me great pain; but what is worse is that I have several others that soon will do the same.

From Signor Rondinelli I hear that the two children of Vincenzio Landucci, for the time being, are under the good care of a woman who took them into her own home a while ago to tend to them: Vincenzio himself was sick with fever, but is feeling better.

I have a wish to know how often our Vincenzio writes to you, Sire.

To respond to that personal detail you shared with me, that you find occupations so salubrious, truly I recognize them as

having that same effect on myself as well: so that even though
the activities occasionally seem superfluous and intolerable to
me, on account of my being a friend of tranquility, I nevertheless see clearly how staying active is the foundation of my
health, and particularly in the time that you have been far away
from us, Sire, with great providence did the Lord arrange it so
that I never had what you might call an hour of peace, thus preventing the oppression of your absence from distressing me.
Such grief would have been harmful to me, and given you cause
for worry instead of the relief I have been able to provide.
Blessed be the Lord, from whom I anticipate new graces for the
future, just as He has granted us so many in the past. Meanwhile, Sire, endeavor to be of good cheer and rely upon the
One who is faithful, just, and merciful, and with Him I leave
you.

Most Beloved Lord Father,
I received your most welcome letter together with the four apricots, which I turned over to La Piera so that she could distribute them to the neighbors. I am greatly cheered to hear that you
go outside the city to take the air, because I know how it sustains and delights you. May it please God that you can come
home soon to enjoy your own little house, the rent for which I
sent this morning to the landlords in the amount of 17 *scudi*
and 1/2, because they were insisting on having it, and I enclose
the list of expenses as well, telling you furthermore how the
blacksmith has returned the 3 barrels of wine that he owed us:
it is of the Navicello variety and good enough for the servants;
thus now we have recovered all that was given, or rather
loaned, to others.

   The white verdea grapes have not yet reached their peak of
perfection, but when they do I will try to acquire some excellent ones, and this man will do us the service of carrying them
to you. I wanted to send you some of the oranges from the garden, but from the sample La Piera brought me I see they are not
quite ready. If good luck had enabled you to find even one gray

partridge or something similar, I would have been thrilled to have it for love of that poor sick young girl, who craves nothing but wild game: at the last full moon she was so ill that she was annointed with holy oil, but now she has made such a comeback that we believe she will live to see the new moon. She speaks with great vivacity, and gulps her food readily, provided we give her tasty things. Last night I stayed with her all through the night, and while I fed her, she said: "I cannot believe that when one stands on the verge of death it is possible to eat the way I do, yet for all that I have no desire to turn back; only to see God's will be done." I pray Him to grant you His holy grace, Sire, and I greet you on behalf of all our friends. From San Matteo in Arcetri, the 18th of November 1633.

Your Most Affectionate Daughter,
SUOR M. CELESTE

Most Beloved Lord Father,
Saturday evening brought me your latest letter, Sire, together with one from Her Ladyship the Ambassadress in Rome, full of loving thanks for the crystal, and condolences upon the deprivation you still endure, Sire, by being barred from returning to your own home. It is surely true that she shows herself to be that same most gracious lady, as you have so often depicted her. I am not sending you her letter because I am uncertain as to whether I must write back to her, but first I will wait to hear what response you may have had from Rome.

I have not failed to conduct a thorough search for the pears you wish, Sire, and I believe I will find something. But because I hear that this year the fruits do not last long, I wonder if it might be better, once I have them, to send them to you right away and not wait for your return, which could be delayed for several more weeks, or so my desire leads me to fear.

Signor Geri shared with us all the fruits from his garden, which were small in number and poor in quality, according to what I hear from Geppo who went to gather them; and he took almost all of the pomegranates for us; though, as I tell you, they are stunted and scant.

Next Sunday we mark the beginning of Advent, wherefore if you will send us the apricots we will be so grateful to have them for the evening meal, but the very plainest ones will suffice us, like those you sent to the neighbors, who join La Piera, she tells me, in thanking you for them and wishing you well; and all of us here do the same while praying Our Lord to bless you.   From San Matteo, the 23rd of November 1633.

Sire's Most Affectionate Daughter,
SUOR MAR. CELESTE

Please turn the page, Sire.

Wednesday at twilight around the twenty-fourth hour, after I had written the other side of this paper, Giovanni appeared here and handed me your letters. It was not possible to send Signor Geri his until the following morning, which I did at a very early hour. Of course I also received the panier containing the 12 thrushes: the additional 4, which would have completed the number you state in your letter, Sire, must have been liberated by some charming little kitten who thought of tasting them ahead of us, because they were not there, and the cloth cover had a large hole in it. How fortunate that the gray partridges and the woodcocks were at the bottom, one of which and two thrushes I gave to the sick girl, to her great joy, and she thanks you, Sire. I sent another gift, also in the form of two thrushes, to Signor Rondinelli, and the remainder we enjoyed together with our friends. I have taken the greatest pleasure in distributing all this among various people, because prizes sought after with such diligence and difficulty deserve to be shared by several, and as the thrushes arrived a little the worse for wear, it was necessary to cook them in a stew, and I stood over them all day, and for once I truly surrendered myself to gluttony.

The news you gave me of the coming of that great Lord and Lady, Sire, was most welcome, as, after word of your own return, I can tell you that I could not possibly receive better tidings; because being so fond of that Lady, and considering how we are obliged to her, I want above all else to meet her in person. Indeed it disturbs me somewhat to hear what a high opinion they both have of me, as I feel certain I will not succeed in expressing with my voice what I have shown of myself by letter. And you well know, Sire, that when it comes to chitchat, or rather I should say discussion, I am good for nothing; but I cannot let these concerns deprive me of a moment's nearness to persons so kind as to indulge me thusly, provided that I can be of service to my dear Lady. Meanwhile I will set about thinking of what gift a poor nun might offer her.

I will be so happy if you can see about getting me some citrons, Sire, because I would not know where to find them, and I recall that Signor Aggiunti sent you several very beautiful ones last year, so that you may be able to try asking him again now, and then I will set myself to work and turn them into candied morsels, extremely delighted to employ myself in this small service for our most illustrious Monsignor, now that I have the grand honor of hearing how these are preferred by His Lordship over all the other confections. I greet you once more, Sire, and pray for your happiness.

Most Beloved Lord Father,
Last Thursday I wrote to you at length, Sire, and now I write again only to tell you that yesterday there came 10 barrels of wine from San Miniato at Todesco. I hear from La Piera that Signor Aggiunti's servant arrived to pour it into the casks; and also that she paid him, though she cannot seem to tell me exactly how much: one cask is completely filled, and I believe it is the one that holds 6 barrels: as for the other of 5 1/2, in order that it not remain half-empty, I told them to finish filling it with the wine they are drinking now, which is reasonably good, but first to draw off several flasks, before the mixing, to top off the cask of 6 barrels. And we will take some, too, because it is light wine, and seems to me to be perhaps a good summer wine for you, Sire; I like the lighter wine at this time of year as well: the

cask that is not mixed will be distinguished by being left alone, and the other will take care of the servants.

This for now is all I need to tell you: I close with the usual loving greetings, and pray Our Lord to keep you.   From San Matteo, the 26th of November 1633.

    Sire's Most Affectionate Daughter,
    SUOR MAR. CELESTE

Most Beloved Lord Father,
I have long known the ineptitude of my ambassador Giovanni; but the desire I had to send for a sight of you, Sire, was the reason I paid no heed to any impediment; all the more so since the Squarcialupi widows granted me the favor of being allowed to employ him for these services; and that is enough said.

Tordo sent yesterday for the 4 *scudi* and had them right away.

Mother Achillea herewith returns the motet. What she would really like in exchange are a few symphonies or ricercar compositions for the organ; you may remember that ours does not function in the high registers, because one or another stop is missing, so that any sonatas to be played upon it would have to be willing to descend very quickly into the low notes.

It does me good to hope, and also to believe firmly, that his Lordship the Ambassador, when he departs from Rome, will be bringing you the news of your dispatch, and also word that he personally will conduct you here in his company. I do not believe that I will live to see that day. May it please the Lord to grant me this grace, if it be for the best; with that thought I greet you with all my love, Sire, and the regards of our usual friends. From San Matteo in Arcetri, the 3rd of December 1633.

    Your Most Affectionate Daughter,
    SUOR M. CELESTE

[On this same day, Ambassador Niccolini wrote to Galileo to say that after five months of negotiations, the pope had finally consented to send him home.]

Most Beloved Lord Father,

Signor Francesco Lupi, the brother-in-law of our Suor Maria Vincenzia, passing through Siena en route to his home in Rome, offered to carry this letter to you, Sire, or anything else I wished to send; wherefore I, accepting the courtesy, offer you this box containing 13 citron candy morsels, for just these many and not one more turned out well from the 6 citrons that Signor Rinuccini sent me, as all of the fruits were small and blemished on one side: their taste I believe will prove excellent, but as for their appearance they could be a bit more beautiful, and would be except that the extremely damp weather obliged me to dry them by the fire. Here, too, is a rose of sugar so that you may see if you would like to have several flowers of this sort to adorn the upside-down cake that we will make for that wedding celebration, Sire, but with flowers much smaller and more delicate than this one.

I received from Master Agostino the box containing the 6 apricots, and I thank you together with those nuns who shared them, who are our usual friends.

I understand that in Florence everyone is saying you will soon be here; but until I have this from your lips, all I will believe is that your dear friends are allowing their affections and desires to give themselves voice. Meanwhile I greatly enjoy hearing that you have such a vibrant complexion, as Master Agostino tells me and further affirms he has never seen you with better color. Everyone can recognize how you have benefited, after the help of blessed God, from the extremely sweet conversation you continue to enjoy with that most illustrious Monsignor Archbishop, as well as from not being careless of your health nor going to extremes as you sometimes do in your own home. Everlasting thanks be offered to the Lord God, for it is He who keeps you in His grace.   From San Matteo in Arcetri, the 9th of December 1633.

Your Most Affectionate Daughter,
SUOR M. CELESTE

Most Beloved Lord Father,
Only a moment before the news of your dispatch reached me, Sire, I had taken my pen in hand to write to Her Ladyship the Ambassadress to beg her once more to intercede in this affair; for having watched it wear on so long, I feared that it might not be resolved even by the end of this year, and thus my sudden joy was as great as it was unexpected: nor are your daughters alone in our rejoicing, but all these nuns, by their grace, give signs of true happiness, just as so many of them have sympathized with me in my suffering. We are awaiting your arrival with great longing, and we cheer ourselves to see how the weather has cleared for your journey.

Signor Geri was leaving this morning with the Court, and I made sure to have him notified before daybreak of your return, Sire; seeing as he had already learned something of the decision, and came here last evening to tell me what he knew. I also explained to him the reason you have not written to him, Sire, and I bemoaned the fact that he will not be here when you arrive to share in our celebration, since he is truly a perfect gentleman, honest and loyal.

I set aside the container of verdea wine, which Signor Francesco could not bring along because his litter was too overloaded. You will be able to send it to the Archbishop later, when the litter makes a return trip: the citron candy morsels I have already consigned to him. The casks for the white wine are all in order.

More I cannot say for the dearth of time, except that all of us send you our loving regards.   From San Matteo, the 10th of December 1633.

Your Most Affectionate Daughter,
Suor M. Celeste

[Galileo returned within days, but the happiness of his homecoming was short-lived. Suor Maria Celeste fell sick three months later and died in the convent the night of April 2 at the age of thirty-three.]

Within a Decade's Correspondence

The dates in this timeline accord with the seventeenth-century Florentine custom Suor Maria Celeste followed, beginning the new year on March 25, the feast of the Annunciation. Some events in Galileo's life, therefore, such as the publication of his *Dialogue* and the wedding of his son, may appear a year premature compared to the dates given in the genealogical chart on page viii or in the text sections of *Galileo's Daughter*.

1623

May: Galileo's sister Virginia dies.

August: Maffeo Cardinal Barberini is elected Pope Urban VIII on the 6th.

September: Galileo's book *The Assayer* is published, dedicated to the new pope. Galileo's son, Vincenzio, enrolls at the University of Pisa.

December: Suor Ortensia del Nente, elected abbess of San Matteo in Arcetri on the 10th, replaces Suor Laura Gaetani.

1624

April: Galileo travels to Rome for papal audience, visiting his patron and publisher, Prince Federico Cesi, en route. Virginio Cesarini, Prince Cesi's young cousin to whom Galileo had dedicated *The Assayer,* dies of tuberculosis.

June: Galileo returns to Florence after six audiences with Urban.

October: Galileo begins work on his *Dialogue on the Two Chief Systems of the World,* continuing on and off over the next six years.

1627

> **July:** Galileo's sister-in-law and her children arrive from Germany for an extended visit.

1628

> **April:** "Aunt Chiara" and her children return to Germany.
> **June:** Vincenzio receives his law degree from Pisa.
> **January:** Vincenzio weds Sestilia Bocchineri of Prato.

1629

> **December:** Galileo completes his *Dialogue on the Two Chief Systems of the World*. Sestilia gives birth to her first child, a boy named Galileo and nicknamed "Galileino." Suor Caterina Angela Anselmi is elected abbess of San Matteo in Arcetri.

1630

> **April:** Galileo travels to Rome to arrange publication of his *Dialogue,* arriving May 3 and staying two months at the Tuscan Embassy.
> **August:** Prince Cesi dies of gangrene of the bladder. Bubonic plague, which entered northern Italy from Germany in 1629, invades Florence.
> **October:** A glassblower of Galileo's dies of plague. Vincenzio and Sestilia flee the city, leaving their baby with Galileo.
> **November:** Suor Violante dies of fever and dysentery. Galileo, constrained by the death of his Roman publisher and the difficulty of inter-city commerce during the plague, finds a new publisher in Florence and turns over his *Dialogue* manuscript to the Florentine Inquisitor. Meanwhile, Galileo begins writing a new book, incorporating much of his life's work and experiments on motion, to be called *Two New Sciences*.
> **January:** Florentine Magistracy of Public Health declares a general quarantine of forty days' duration. Galileo's brother, Michelangelo, dies in Germany. Sestilia gives birth to Galileo's second grandson, Carlo.
> **March:** Galileo receives permission from Rome to publish his *Dialogue*.

1631

May: Vincenzio Landucci sues Galileo (his uncle) for his monthly living expenses. Suor Maria Celeste begins helping her father look for a house in Arcetri.

June: Printing of Galileo's *Dialogue* begins.

September: Galileo moves from Bellosguardo to Arcetri, taking a rented villa around the corner from the convent.

November: Vincenzio and Sestilia move with their children to Poppi, where he is employed as a chancellor, and Sestilia's brothers occupy their home on the Costa San Giorgio.

February: *Dialogue* printing is completed and a copy presented to the Grand Duke.

1632

May: Galileo sends copies of his *Dialogue* to Rome with a traveling friend.

August: Hostile reactions to the *Dialogue* stir Pope Urban's anger in Rome.

September: Orders reach the Inquisitor at Florence that the *Dialogue* can no longer be sold in that city. The original manuscript, copied in part by Suor Maria Celeste, is sent from Florence to Rome in compliance with official request. Galileo is summoned to Rome by the Inquisition.

October: Galileo appeals the summons, unsuccessfully.

November: Galileo falls ill, unable to travel.

December: Suor Lucrezia Santini is elected abbess of San Matteo.

January: Galileo leaves for Rome on the 20th.

February: Galileo arrives at the Tuscan Embassy on the 13th, after two weeks in quarantine at Acquapendente.

1633

April: Galileo testifies before the Holy Office on the 12th and the 30th, remaining in an apartment in the Palace of the Holy Office between interrogations. A private interview with the Commissary General on the 28th leads Galileo to believe he will emerge unscathed from the proceedings.

May: Galileo testifies a third time on the 10th and tenders his formal, written defense. The Madonna of Impruneta is carried through the streets of Florence from the 20th through the 23rd.

June: Galileo is sentenced on the 22nd and his *Dialogue* banned.

July: Galileo, still under arrest, is transferred to the custody of the Archbishop of Siena.

August: Galileo's sentence is read aloud to all mathematicians and philosophers in Florence. He resumes work on *Two New Sciences*.

September: Florentine health officials declare the city free of plague on the 17th.

December: Galileo returns to his villa in Arcetri under perpetual house arrest.

1634

April: Suor Maria Celeste dies at the convent.

The Sisters of San Matteo
(a partial list)

Suor Achillea
Suor Arcangela Galilei
Suor Barbara
Suor Brigida
Suor Cammilla
Suor Caterina Angiola Anselmi
Suor Cherubina
Suor Chiara Landucci
Suor Clarice Burci
Suor Diamante
Suor Giulia Corso
Suor Elisabetta (Lisabetta) Gherardini
Suor Isabella
Suor Laura Gaetani
Suor Lucrezia Santina
Suor Luisa Pitti
Suor Maria Celeste Galilei
Suor Maria Grazia Del Pace
Suor Maria Maddalena Squadrini
Suor Maria Silvia Boscoli
Suor Maria Teodora Ninci
Suor Maria Vincenzia
Suor Maria Virginia Castrucci
Suor Oretta
Suor Ortensa del Nente
Suor Polissena Vinta
Suor Prudenza
Suor Smeralda
Suor Violante Rondinelli
Suor Virginia Canigiani

Florentine Weights, Measures, & Currency

WEIGHT

libbra = 12 *oncie* = .75 pound = .3 kilogram (plural is *libbre*)

LINEAR MEASURE

braccio = about 23 inches (plural is *braccia*)

DRY MEASURE

staio = 1 bushel
moggio = 24 bushels

LIQUID MEASURE

fiasco = 4 pints
barile = 20 *fiaschi* = 10 gallons

CURRENCY

scudo = 7 *lire*
piastra = 22.42 grams of silver = about 5 *lire*
lira (silver coin) = 10 *quattrini* = 12 *crazie* = 20 *soldi*
   (Four *lire* could feed one person for a week.)
giulio (silver coin) = slightly more than half a *lira* = 13 *soldi*
quattrino = .1 *lira* = 2 *soldi*